Waves of Grace

Experiences of Devotees

Waves of Grace

Experiences of Devotees

Published by:
Mata Amritanandamayi Center
P.O. Box 613
San Ramon, CA 94583-0613, USA
Tel: 001 510 537 9417
Website: www.amma.org

First Edition, October 2017

Waves of Grace

Experiences of Devotees

Mata Amritanandamayi Center, San Ramon
California, United States

O Amma...

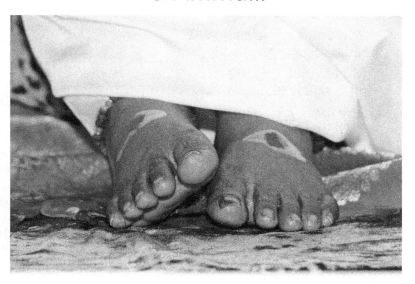

*...may the waves of divine grace
anoint our lives and take us to You.*

CONTENTS

Preface   10

New Horizons

"What do you want?"   14
Dhanya Vingadassamy, Réunion Island

"You came to help!"   17
Shanti Jayaraj, Australia

"My Mama!"   22
Esther Mueni Wambua, Kenya

"She listens to everyone..."   26
I.C. Dave, India

"You are my very own!"   31
Lakshmi, India

"My darling son..."   37
Animon, India

"This kid looks like my son!"   42
Cecile Villacampa Toubal, Spain

Rite of Passage

Mother of Liberty   49
Aswathi, USA

Uplifted   59
Vijaykumar, India

A Painful Lesson   66
O. Sham Bhat, India

New Lease on Life 71
Rahul Menon, India

Transfiguration 75
VSK, India

Welcome Back to Life 80
Rebekka Roininen, Finland

That Cigarette Stub 87
Indira, India

Anointment

Divine Grace 92
MKR, India

True Payasam 97
Ahalya (Maila Korhonen), Finland

Magic Touch 106
Andrew Bukraba, Australia

Mysterious Messenger 110
Satish Kumar V., India

All-knowing Mother 114
Amit Kadam, India

Divine Protection 120
N. Vasudevan, Nigeria

Mata Pita Press 126
Lalitha Unny, India

Anointed with Love 132
Sharadamani, India

Saving Grace

Healed by Amma   138
Yusuf Husayn Abdullah, UK

Saving Grace   142
Swapna Dayanandan, Singapore

Gift of Fate   148
Prem, India

Watching Over Us   152
Santosh (Sunny Nell), USA

My Secret   157
M. Ramakrishnan, USA

Primordial Doctor   161
Dr. V. Satyaprasad, India

Rebirth   164
E. Shanta Krishnankutty, India

When Amma Says Something   170
Ashok Nair, Qatar

Meeting the Mata   176
Aftab Ahmed, India

Blessed Journey

Maverick   183
Sugunanandan-acchan, India

Over Gleaming Embers   199
Kasturibai, India

Blessed Journey   211
Satheesh Idamannel, India

"I taught Amma!"   219
Selin Rodrigues, India

My Amma   224
Rajan Maestri, India

First Impressions   231
Sethuraman Srinivas Kuruvimalai, U.S.A.

Engaged for Eternity   237
Rehana Raj T., India

"Amma's still the same!"   247
Priyan (Fouad Nassif), Lebanon

The Crossing

My Mother   259
Br. Eknath, India

Visitation from Amma   268
Madhuree Biswas, India

Boundless Compassion   274
Bri. Niranjanamrita Chaitanya, India

Never Too Late   280
Madhavi (Raymonde Binner), U.S.A.

Glossary   288

Preface

Samsara — the ceaseless flow of existence, characterized by the swirl of worldly life and by the cycle of birth, death and rebirth — is often likened to a sea. A seeker of Truth must cross this vast realm of transmigration in order to attain *moksha*, spiritual liberation. The key to a successful crossing is *ishwara kripa*, God's grace.

How does one earn kripa? By clinging to God, the way a monkey clings to its mother? Or, as with a young kitten, by allowing the Divine Mother to pick one up by the scruff of one's neck, as it were? By being both the monkey *and* kitten, i.e. by striving and surrendering, for they are different phases of the journey to God.

Amma says as much. She defines the word *'ashram'* (generally translated as 'monastery') as *"aa shramam"* — "that effort" (one makes to reach the spiritual goal). From this, it is clear that She endorses *sadhana* (spiritual striving). However, Amma time and again stresses that more than human effort, what one needs is divine grace.

What exactly is grace? It is the X-factor that crowns struggle with success. It manifests as the noble impulse to do good and to turn Godward. Though intangible, kripa is palpable, as legions of devotees will affirm. This book is a testament to the waves of divine grace that have anointed their pilgrimage through life.

Amma's is a larger than life presence, whose auspicious influence sometimes makes itself felt even before one meets Her. *Waves of Grace* begins with stories of those who encountered Amma before physically meeting Her, encounters that unveiled new horizons in their spiritual lives.

For most seekers, the spiritual life is not lived in a cloister, rather the mainstream of worldly life, with its trials and tribulations. The silver lining behind these darks clouds is the Guru, whose luminous guidance and grace redeem Her followers from suffering and give meaning and hope to their lives. The pages that follow include accounts of how Amma's words of wisdom infused in Her children the strength to bear their lot, and of how Her saving grace delivered them from the ravages of illness, addiction and other misfortunes.

That said, one must never imagine that the sole aim of spirituality is to help one skirt life's treacherous shoals. It is not a form of escapism, as Amma often reminds us. On the contrary, it is the assimilation of principles that will help us squarely face both the good and bad with equanimity. The most immutable fact of life is mortality. Some of the most poignant stories here are of those who have had to face the death of their loved ones, and who have done so without keeling over.

In the fathomless depths of the ocean of samsara lie precious gems, and one can gather these pearls of peace and jewels of spiritual wisdom through pure love for the divine. Many share how Amma has enriched their lives with the priceless treasures of devotion, selflessness and compassion.

This book is a distillation of the many experiences of divine grace that devotees from all walks of life and all corners of the world have shared over the last 30 years or so through the pages of *Matruvani*, the ashram's flagship publication. Many, many thanks to all of them. A big thank you to Dayakaran Hirtenstein for painstakingly gathering and scanning many issues of *Matruvani*, especially the older ones. Thanks also to Vimalkumar, who painted the remarkable illustrations of Amma used in the book. Last but not least, special thanks to Swami Amritaswarupananda Puri, Veena O'Sullivan and Jyotsna Lamb for their invaluable editorial input and constructive feedback. *Om amriteshwaryai namah.*

Br. Satish

New Horizons

"What do you want?"

Dhanya Vingadassamy, Réunion Island

I was born on the island of Réunion near Mauritius. My father was of Indian origin, whereas my mother was of Indo-Chinese origin. I was baptized and brought up in the Christian faith. While still a child, I used to pray to and confide in the Holy Virgin Mary. I would relate all my childish worries to Her while adorning Her altar in the church with flowers. She was the compassionate Mother, who not only listened to me but understood me as well.

I got married late in life. My husband was not at all interested in spirituality, but with God's grace, I was able to bring him to the spiritual path. In 1970, three years after our marriage, my first child was born. From day one, he was desperately ill. His chances of survival were practically nil. When he was four days old, doctors started giving him blood transfusions. This went on for months. I prayed fervently to the Divine Mother, making many vows in the hope that doing so would save my child's life.

One night in 1971, I dreamt of a radiant woman dressed in brightly colored Indian clothes. She was full of light. I clearly saw a luminous aura around Her crowned head. I had never seen Her before. Taking my child and me into Her arms, She asked, "What do you want?" I replied that I wanted my child to be healthy.

The miracle happened almost instantly. My child recovered completely. My husband was puzzled. He asked me to narrate the dream to him in detail and to describe the radiant woman. The doctors were even more baffled as there was suddenly no need for blood transfusions any more. My faith in the Divine Mother grew stronger, and I continued to pray to Her.

In 1978, when I was pregnant with my second child, there was an enormous, benign tumor in my womb that made the pregnancy difficult. One day, after I had returned home from work, I lay down in my room. Suddenly, at the window, I saw the same divine form I had seen in my dream a few years before. She smiled at me. My husband, who was also in the room, saw nothing. He became scared when he saw my face. This vision lasted for no more than a few seconds. Despite the tumor, my second child was born healthy. Six months later, I underwent an operation to remove the tumor.

In 1982, I met Br. Madhu by chance. He spoke to me about Amma, and gave me a small photo of Her. He suggested that I keep the picture in the house and place a flower at Her feet. I was very attracted to the photo. From then on, I started praying to Amma while saying my regular prayers. I would look at the photo and speak to Her. Br. Madhu, who later became Swami Premananda, used to visit our house. We all prayed together and celebrated Amma's birthdays. Little by little, things changed in my life. I became close to Amma. My spiritual practices also deepened.

In 1987, Amma visited Réunion for the first time. I had the opportunity to meet Her at the airport when She disembarked from the plane. That was my very first darshan. Although it was the first time I was meeting Her, I had the feeling that I had known Her for a long time.

During the first Devi Bhava at the Saint Louis Ashram in Réunion, Amma held me in Her arms. It was then that I relived the dream I had had 16 years before, in 1971. Mother was dressed in the same manner, and She looked at me in exactly the same way She had looked at me in the dream. And then, to my astonishment, She asked me the same thing that She had then, "What do you want?" Tears started rolling down my cheeks because I knew then that before me was the Mother whom I had been praying to all those years — the Universal Mother, the embodiment of Love and Compassion.

(May 1999)

"You came to help!"

Shanti Jayaraj, Australia

I am of Sri Lankan origin, but have lived in Australia for many years. I have three daughters, one of whom is a special-needs child who requires a great deal of care. I consider that daughter, Yarlini, a special gift from God.

She was born in Sri Lanka on March 29th, 1980, and suffered from epilepsy from the time she was born. She used to have five or six seizures every day. She was only 14 days old when she was first given medication to prevent her condition, but the medication had no effect.

When Yarlini was 18 months old, we met a doctor in Sri Lanka who helped stop her seizures with indigenous medicine. Nevertheless, Yarlini still needed everything to be done for her. Well into her childhood, she remained like a baby, both physically and mentally. The biggest problem, however, was that she never wanted to sleep at night. We tried all kinds of medication to change her sleeping pattern, but nothing worked. As she couldn't talk, she wasn't able to tell us what she was feeling or what she wanted. This went on for nearly 12 years.

I was blessed to have a family that helped to care for Yarlini, especially during the nights, because she always wanted someone with her. We prayed continually for the extra energy we needed to carry on.

17

Though it was not easy, I felt that God had entrusted us with a special duty. When I felt frustrated, I would console myself with the thought that I had been born to look after this special soul. Whenever I prayed, I would tell God, "I am only her baby-sitter. You are her real mother. If You don't care for Your own daughter, no one will. All that I ask of You is that You give me the extra strength I need to take care of her."

Though I had faith in God, I never had any faith in Gurus. I felt it was not necessary to pray to a human form when I could communicate with God directly and surrender all my problems to Him. I never thought He could assume a human form.

One night in August 1989, I was taking care of Yarlini as usual. She finally fell asleep at about 3:30 a.m. By that time, I was very tired. I lay down beside Yarlini and fell asleep.

At about 5:30 a.m., I woke up to the sound of someone opening the bedroom door. When I looked up, I saw a woman in a white sari. The sari was tied across her chest, and the rest of the cloth draped down her left arm. Her sari was dripping wet. Her hair was tied in a bun on top of her head. She was dark and well-built. She came to me and said, "I've taken my bath. I will look after your daughter. You can go and sleep now."

I got up quietly and went to my room. I felt neither fear of this woman nor curiosity about who she was. But as soon as I reached my room, I came to my senses: I realized I had left my daughter with a stranger. I rushed back to the room with my husband, but the woman wasn't there. Yarlini was sleeping peacefully. I knew it had definitely not been a dream. It was, as I would later realize, a vision.

I immediately called one of my best friends in Perth, and later, my mother, in Sri Lanka. They were both happy for me. Although the experience had been most vivid, it faded with the passing of time.

Two years after this experience, I became an active member of the Hindu Temple Association of Western Australia. During one of the meetings, I met a man, who said that his Guru had graciously agreed to visit Western Australia. He asked the committee members if we could help him arrange his Guru's programs and find a house close to the Hindu temple to ac-commodate his Guru and the group accompanying her.

Though I had never believed in Gurus, for some reason, I felt that I should help. I offered the man my home, saying that if it was good enough for his Guru and her group, I would be happy to let them use it. My family would make alternative living ar-rangements during that period. When the man consequently visited my home, I intuitively sensed that his Guru should stay with us. I told him that I felt I was blessed. Before leaving, he gave me a video tape and asked me to watch it, so that I could see whom I was going to accommodate.

When I watched the video, to my astonishment, I saw that the Guru was the stranger who had come to my house two years before! I started crying. From the bottom my heart, I prayed to Her: "I never came in search of You. And yet, You came to help me. I have to see You! O Amma, please don't disappoint me! Please make it possible!" My prayer was answered.

It would be several months before Amma came to Australia. My husband and I felt we couldn't wait that long. So, in May 1992, we made plans to visit Amma in Amritapuri.

After we landed in Chennai, which was still a considerable distance from Amritapuri, we discovered to our great surprise that Amma was in Chennai then, giving darshan at Her ashram there. As Yarlini was with us, I felt grateful to Amma for making it easy for us to meet Her.

Amma's Devi Bhava darshan took place during Her last program in Chennai. It was midnight by the time we had our darshan. Amma asked us for a piece of sandalwood, which She would bless; we were to apply the paste on Yarlini's forehead every night when she went to bed.

Where were we to find sandalwood in the middle of the night? We needed to get it right away as Amma was returning to Amritapuri the next day, and we were leaving India.

A man in the darshan queue overheard us. He said that he had a piece of sandalwood in his house, and that he would get it right away. He said that the sandalwood had simply been lying in a cupboard for several months. As he left, I was stunned by how Amma had reserved that piece of sandalwood for us in someone else's cupboard all that time. She blessed the sandalwood and gave it to us. She also autographed a *bhajan* book (book of devotional songs in praise of God), writing in Malayalam: 'May divine peace guide my darling children. Loving kisses from Amma!'

From that day onwards, we saw a great change in our daughter's sleeping pattern. By Amma's grace, Yarlini now sleeps by herself every night.

I feel that Amma is none other than the Divine Mother Herself. We are blessed to have met Her. May She dwell permanently in the hearts of all.

(October 1999)

"My Mama!"

Esther Mueni Wambua, Kenya

I have experienced Amma's infinite power and the flood of Her compassion.

In 2006, I fell sick and was admitted at the Pine Breeze Hospital in Nakuru. For a week, I was in a coma. The doctors carried out many tests but couldn't find out what the problem was. My family members were worried. They thought I was bewitched and dying, and thus gave up on me.

On the seventh day, at around 2 a.m., I felt the healing touch of some unknown energy. I saw someone before me wearing a red sari. I could not see the face properly because of the sheer brightness surrounding it. I came to a sitting position; I don't know how I did it or where I was. The being came near me; I could now see clearly that it was a woman. I asked who She was and what She wanted. She told me that She was my Mama (Mother) and that She had come so that I could be healed. She then hugged me, and I felt my inner joy rising steadily. I was trembling and I said to Her, "If you are the Supreme Master, you know me well. You know I have no will power left. I have absolutely no confidence in myself."

She said to me, "Be not dismayed, for I will help you. I will strengthen and uphold you."

All this time, I was in Her loving arms. She then vanished.

When the doctors and my family came in the morning, they were stunned to find me out of bed. Nobody believed my story, apart from my mother and brother.

Five years later, I was employed at the Sher Karuturi Farm. Our boss provided free transport for everyone who wished to go to Nairobi to receive darshan from Her Holiness Sri Mata Amritanandamayi Devi.

When I stepped into the temple, I was shocked to see the same woman I had seen in that vision five years before. I had no doubts She was the one because I experienced the same feelings as before. I realized that fate had led me to the Sher Karuturi Farm, so that I could see my loving Mother.

The queue was long, and though I was moving closer to Mother, it was getting late. Our driver ordered us to go back to the bus so that we could reach the farm before it was late. I was disappointed that I had to leave before getting darshan. I pleaded with the driver, in vain.

When I heard that Amma was visiting the area near the farm, I wanted to go and see Her but was denied permission. I decided to sneak out from my work place but the gateman asked for my gate pass, which I didn't have. I was left with no choice but to return to work. I was so angry that I didn't want to talk to anyone.

On the seventh night after seeing Amma, I had another vision of Her. I wrote down some of the things She said to me:

1. We will never know where we stand until Amma shows us. Only when She sheds light in our heart and shows us as She sees us will we ever know ourselves as we truly are.

2. If we steer our lives according to Amma's guidance, we will be saved, but if we follow our own inclinations, our lives will get wrecked.

3. Our culture, social position or reputation does not matter. Unless we face the great issue of our spiritual condition with utmost earnestness and seriousness, we are playing the fool.

4. Be honest with yourself, your fellowmen, and with God.

Since then, my heart has been at peace with everyone. And since that day, the voice of Her Holiness has been the sweetest music to me. I've known no greater joy than that of glad communion with Amma.

In August, my sister called me at 2 a.m. to say that her baby had stopped breathing. She was crying. I asked to talk to my mother, who was also crying. I wasn't frightened at all because I knew that Amma was in control. I remembered what She had told me five years ago: "Be not dismayed, for I will help you. I will strengthen and uphold you." I took a picture of Amma and embraced it. I don't know how long I lay there, holding the picture. After some time, the phone rang; it was my sister — her baby was well. I thanked Amma for always being there for us.

Amma is worthy of our faith, and of the surrender of our intellect, our doubts and emotions, and our will. I just want to tell Amma, "I surrender myself to You."

My yoga teacher Sunil Khallungal and my boss Nagesh Karuturi have helped me realize that my feelings for Amma are genuine, and that I am not insane, as some of my fellow Christians think. Now I want to meet Amma face to face, and open my heart to Her. May the full glory of Amma be unveiled to the whole universe. May I discover Her divine presence within me. I want to be Amma's child, servant, worshipful devotee, disciple and a shadow ever trailing Her.

(March 2011)

"She listens to everyone..."
I.C. Dave, India

One day, while working in my lab, I received a phone call from my friend, Dr. P.K. Bhattacharya, who is Head of the Radiation Department, Bhabha Atomic Research Centre, Mumbai. He told me that he had just returned from Russia, and wanted to tell me about an incident that would interest me greatly. When I went to see him, he said, "I had an opportunity to work with scientists from the Atomic Research Centre of Siberia (Russia), and it was a good experience. But what I am eager to tell you about is the unusual experience I heard from one of the Russian scientists there. That's why I called you.

"When I arrived at Irkutsk Airport, Dr. Mikhailovich came to receive me. As he approached me, I was wonderstruck by what I saw: 'Amma' pictures in both pockets of his coat. Who wouldn't be surprised to see photos of Amma in the pockets of an atomic scientist in Siberia? I immediately asked him, 'Those are photos of Amma, aren't they?'

"He said, 'Yes.'

"After we completed the immigration formalities and got into the car, I asked him, 'Where did you meet Amma?'

"To my surprise, he said that he has not seen Amma. I asked him many questions. What he narrated is as follows:

"'I've been doing research in atomic science here for the last 10 years. A few years ago, I got married to the daughter of one of my professors. We now have a sweet little daughter, who is three years old. I had differences of opinion with my wife, and they increased after our daughter's birth. One of the reasons for this was that my wife considered herself superior to me because she was my professor's daughter. She just couldn't forget that. Finally, she left me, and returned to her father's house, taking my daughter with her. Two-and-a-half years passed, and yet, I was not prepared for a divorce because I loved my wife and daughter deeply. Being a communist, I had no faith in God.

"'One day, I came across an article in Russian, in a Russian magazine, about a woman saint from India, Sri Mata Amrita-nandamayi Devi. A few sentences from that article made a great impact on me, and they changed my life. That paragraph went something like this:

> There is something special about this woman saint, who is known all over the whole world as 'Amma.' Anyone can talk to Her directly and personally. She listens to every-one attentively, whether that person is in front of Her or thousands of miles away from Her; whether that person has met Her or not.

"'I was astounded. Ordinarily, I would have laughed at such statements, but at that time, I was feeling depressed and helpless. Those words aroused hope in me, and I had full faith in them. Thereafter, I started conversing with Amma. I would talk to Her every day, imagining that She was sitting in front of me. With tearful eyes, I shared the sorrows of my heart with Her. Gradually, I started feeling Her presence, and felt that She was listening to me. Sometimes, I would cry loudly and my prayers became more fervent.

"'After about 15 days, my internal conversation with Amma bore fruit. My wife called me and confessed that she had gone astray because of her ego. She realized and regretted her mistake and wanted to come back to me.

"'My joy was boundless. We were reunited and now my life is filled with joy and peace.

"'After this experience, I had an intense desire to meet Amma, but I had no idea how and where I could meet Her. I made inquiries through that Russian magazine, and I was given the address of the Sri Mata Amritanandamayi Seva Samiti in Moscow. I contacted the organization, which sent me detailed information about Amma, as well as Her photos.

"'It is Amma who reunited me with my wife and daughter. I always keep Her photo close to my heart. Not only during the day, even at night, I go to sleep with Amma's photo close to my heart.'"

When I heard this story, I was dumbfounded. I realized that Amma is all-pervading. She dwells in the heart of every being.

That is how She is able to hear the prayers of everyone from everywhere in the world. She makes no distinctions of religion, caste, language, country or distance. The mere fact that this incident, which took place in far-off Russia, reached me without the help of any media, but through a trustworthy person like Dr. Bhattacharya is also an example of Amma's immense power.

Thereafter, during one of Amma's Delhi programs, I had the opportunity to give an introductory speech about Amma. I narrated Dr. Mikhailovich's experience on that occasion.

The next day, Amma's program had been arranged at the Shankar Math. There, when Amma was giving darshan to devotees, a gentleman came up to me and started speaking in a voice heavy with emotion. "Yesterday, I heard from you the experience of the Russian scientist, and today, I, too, had a miraculous experience!"

Curious, I asked, "Would you mind sharing your experience with me?"

He said, "Today, when I was in Amma's embrace, tears started flowing profusely from my eyes. Amma asked me why I was crying. I couldn't say anything, for my throat was choked with emotion. Tears of joy flowed endlessly. For the last two years, I have been suffering from acute depression, to use the language of psychology. Anyone with this illness loses interest in life. Having lost all hope in life, one develops strong suicidal tendencies. Yesterday, after hearing Dr. Mikhailovich's experience, I, too, started an inner conversation with Amma. Within a day, I received an opportunity to see Her. What a blessing! In those invaluable moments when She hugged me, I was wholly cured of my illness."

Tears of gratitude were flowing from his eyes. I expressed my skepticism. "Sir, you say that Amma's hug cured you of acute depression. Couldn't this be a delusion? Only a psychiatrist can certify that you have been cured."

His answer stunned me. He said, "I can say with full confidence that I am free from it because I am a psychiatrist. I had a practice in the U.S. for 15 years. For the last few years, I have been practicing in Delhi."

I asked him politely, "May I narrate your experience in Amma's programs?"

"Why not?" he said. "You can also mention my name: Dr. Vimal Kshetrapal, M.D. (Psychiatry)."

He said in a devotion-filled voice, "Amma is the Psychiatrist of psychiatrists."

(December 2012)

"You are my very own!"
Lakshmi, India

A young mother was begging in a crowded street corner. She was clutching her four children, who were wailing stubbornly, unable to contain their hunger pangs. I was the eldest child. My name is Lakshmi. Who gave me that name? My father, Mohanan, or my mother, Leena? I was seven then. I had two younger brothers, Vijayan and Kumaran. My little sister, who was always in my mother's arms, was called Girija.

All the money my mother acquired through begging, my father would squander in drinks. All that we received were his kicks.

One evening, my mother and I were moving with out-stretched arms in a crowded corner of the city when someone threw boiling water on my mother. I saw her reel in pain and collapse.

Another time, goaded by hunger and thirst, I leaned too far into a well and fell into it. I remember the faces of the strangers who pulled me out (I wished then that they hadn't) and gathered around me, sighing in sympathy.

Even though I try to forget all these painful experiences, the memories come unbidden. In trying to pen them down, I don't know where or how to begin. I don't even know when or where I was born. Do street beggars know such things?

My earliest memory is of a hut on some wasteland. Having lost all sense because of his excessive drinking, my father had lately been beating my mother mercilessly. He then walked out, taking my two younger brothers with him. Girija and I were left with our mother. Did they divide their only assets, their children? I don't know. The only thing I know for sure is that the last walk my mother took me and my sister on was supposed to be our tryst with death.

We reached a deserted beach. The sand was scorching hot. I was close behind my mother as she walked into the water. When she was knee deep, she paused for a moment. As the next wave came roaring in, she lifted Girija, who was on her hip, and hurled her far into the blue waters. As I stood there gaping, not knowing what to do, she grabbed my arm and pulled me forcibly away towards the shore, not turning back to look even once.

I kept looking back until we were too far away from the beach. I hoped to God that a snow-white bird might come flying, and lift my little sister to safety.

My accursed mother then walked towards the railway tracks, pulling me along. As I couldn't follow her, I was soon left behind. Suddenly, the sight of my mother was obliterated by the train that rushed past with a deafening roar. That was the last time I saw her.

"Street beggar woman dies after being hit by train," the police must have recorded.

One of the many people who gathered to gaze at the gruesome scene on the rails took my arm and walked off. What he wanted was a servant. When he and his family eventually realized that I was unfit for physical work, they brought me to Amritaniketan, Amma's orphanage in Parippally, Kollam. They left me there, saying they would return a few days later but I never saw them again.

I arrived at the orphanage a few days before Onam, Kerala's harvest festival. The love and attention I received here was a new experience for me. Over the next few days, some of the children were taken home by their relatives for Onam. No one came for me. Only a few of us remained at the orphanage.

I asked one of those children, "Will anyone be coming to take you home?"

"No," she said.

"Aren't you sad?" I asked.

Smiling, the girl took my hand and said, "Why should we be sad? We are all going to the ashram to see Amma. Amma will feed us special Onam dishes. She will make us sit in a swing and rock us with Her own hands. She will sing and dance with us. She will shower kisses on each of us." As she was describing all that Amma would do, her face was radiant with joy.

At that time, I hardly knew anything about Amma, whose photos I had seen in the office and classrooms of Amritanik-etan. Most of the residents would pray with joined palms before the photos. Would this Amma, whom my friend was raving about, really give me that much love?

We reached Amritapuri a few days before Onam. We entered the prayer hall and joined the long queue for Amma's darshan. As we slowly moved closer to Amma, my mind was filled with questions. How would Amma receive me? Would She also reject me, as life seemed to have until then? If Amma forsakes me, where would I go?

When I reached Her lap, Amma whispered affectionately, "My pearl, my darling daughter, do not worry. Isn't Amma with you?"

Amma's voice was laden with such sweet love as I had never experienced before. I burst into tears. I wanted to shout, "I'm no longer an orphan! I'm no longer a beggar!"

I had always been nagged by the fear that as the child of a beggar woman, I would have to spend my life begging in the streets, or face an even worse fate. The words Amma whispered in my ear gave me hope, confidence and an indescribable joy.

I used to satisfy my hunger with food from garbage bins. Now, Amma was feeding me good food on a clean plate. I used to wear dirty, discarded clothes. Amma gave me beautiful, colored garments. Amma also taught me the first letters of the

Malayalam alphabet. Those who came for Amma's darshan that day may remember this. She made me stand close to Her. In between darshans, She took my finger and wrote on the slate the first letter, 'A,' in Malayalam, while saying it aloud. She would then give me back the slate and continue giving darshan. After I had written this letter many times on the slate, She would stop darshan for a moment, take the slate again, and write the next letter, 'Aa.' She would then return the slate to me and continue giving darshan. I feel so blessed that the Divine Mother, the Goddess of Learning Herself, who is revered by millions, initiated me into learning. I can honestly say that, more than tears of sorrow and suffering, I have now shed more tears thinking of Mother's love and compassion.

Memories of the crashing waves thumping the beach, the roaring train hurtling past, and the forms of my younger brothers who walked away holding my father's hands sometimes create a sickening pain in my heart. At such times, Amma assuages the pain with special words of consolation.

Would you be pleased if a seven-year-old girl with unkempt hair and dirty clothes touched your arm in a bus or train or on a crowded footpath and called you "Mother?" No. None of those whom I had touched and called "Mother" liked it. In their eyes, there was only revulsion or contempt. How often I used to wish that someone would smile at me and lovingly put his or her hand on my head!

Amma changed my destiny. How many times has She drawn me to Her bosom and whispered into my ear, "Darling daughter, you are my very own!" How many times has Amma wiped away my tears with Her own sari!

I have found my real Mother. She must be yours, too.

(August 2001)

"My darling son..."
Animon, India

Many years ago, when I entered the precincts of what is now called Amritaniketan, the orphanage was not managed by the Mata Amritanandamayi Math. I entered the building, holding my mother's hand. I was feeling completely lost and started crying, but my mother paid no heed to it. She forcefully detached her hand and walked away. A teacher roughly took hold of my hand and dragged me into a classroom. She looked at me with contempt, as if to say, "One more wretch has arrived!" My memories begin from that time.

I gathered myself and looked around the classroom. There was a blackboard on three legs, a board in such bad shape that nothing much was visible on it. Someone had inscribed dull, lifeless letters on it. I looked at the children, who were staring at me in wonder. Their eyes were sunken. Their hair had not seen oil for ages. Their clothes looked as if they had never been washed. Some of them were covered with sores and itches. I looked at the teacher. There was no light or love in her eyes; no smile on her lips. Her face was covered with talcum powder, and there was a sticker *bindi* on her forehead. I caught whiffs of perfume. I felt too scared to approach her. If only she had smiled, if only she had called me "Son..." If only... if only... I was hungry for love and affection.

I can never forget the doctor and nurse from the local government hospital who came periodically to conduct perfunctory check-ups. The doctor's face itself was frightening. We were terrified more about his visits than by any disease! Before we could completely tell him about our illness, he would have finished writing a prescription, torn it from the pad, and thrust it into our hands. And in a language we did not understand, he would call out, "Next..."

The place was infested with anti-social elements. Some people would gather to gamble. Others would drink. We were petrified. The persons responsible for us would pretend to sleep. We were a burden they did not want to shoulder.

It was then that we heard that 'Amma' was taking over the orphanage. By mid-1989, the M.A. Math had officially taken over the orphanage. Soon, people arrived to take care of us and to give us good clothes and proper food. These brahmacharis (male disciples) from the ashram were angels. They gave us perfumed soap, tasty food, and good, clean clothes. We began losing the sense that we were orphans.

A lot of development work took place soon thereafter. New buildings with new facilities began to sprout. Many people worked hard under Amma's guidance to develop this orphanage. In both 1989 and 1990, we won first prize in the *pancha-vadyam*[1] competition at the state-level schools' cultural meet. In 1991 and 1992, Amritaniketan students won second prize.

I was fortunate enough to lead the teams. Today, the Amrita Sanskrit Higher Secondary School and the adjacent Amritaniketan are forces to reckon with in the field of education.

We, the orphans — forgotten and ignored by the world — gained a Mother, who is an ocean of love and compassion. Most of us had imagined that there was nothing for us beyond the walls of this orphanage, and that we would be battered and bruised when we went out into the big, wide world. Amma entered this dismal world of ours, and gave us refuge in Her lap. I unburdened all my sorrows in that loving lap. Amma placed Her left hand on my shoulder and wiped away my tears with Her right hand. Time and again, She consoled me, "Don't, my dear child, don't be sad... Amma is here for you. Amma is with you, my darling son..." The tears of sorrow gave way to an immense sense of gratitude to Amma. Our lives started afresh, renewed with hope, faith and optimism. Amma, the very personification of universal motherhood, was and is so completely alert to our needs. When I think about this, I always feel that, even though I was accursed, orphaned and destitute, carrying the burdensome *prarabdha* (consequences of actions done in previous lives) of my sinful past, Amma has lifted me above all that. She gathered us — the scum of society, living in

---

1 Traditional instrumental ensemble comprising five instruments, typically performing in temples and/or festivals in Kerala

the abysmal byways of an indifferent world, and destined to feed only on leftovers — clasped us tenderly, embraced us, and infused a new hope and vitality into our lives.

After finishing my 10th standard, I was again in a dilemma. What next, I wondered with a shudder? Amma graciously blessed me by offering me a job in the orphanage itself. After a few months, when I went to the ashram for darshan, Amma made me sit near Her. After some time, She looked at me and asked, "Son, what are you doing with your salary? How do you spend it?"

I was dumbfounded. I began to sob. Looking at me, Amma continued, "Will you go back to your old friends and squander your money away by smoking and gambling?" Her words were moist with the essence of a mother's love, one who is anxious about the future of her son, and who wishes him a bright future. She then said, "Son, open a bank account. Save half your salary every month. Send the rest to your house in Chittar."

I follow Amma's instructions even today. Once a year, I visit my house to meet my relatives. Then I see my old friends. They lead a miserable life, addicted to liquor and drugs — men with emaciated bodies, bloodshot eyes, and three to four children each. They are progressing steadily from one hell to another. I don't even stay there for a whole day.

A few months ago, when I went to receive *prasad* (consecrated offering) from Amma, She said loudly, in a playful manner, "Isn't it time to get married?"

I was completely taken aback and felt abashed. I folded my hands and gave my stock answer to such questions, "Please do not yoke this bullock! I wish to continue like this." Amma burst out laughing!

I have only one desire: to serve in any of Amma's institutions, doing any work I can. I know the agony of poverty and the pangs of terrible hunger. By Amma's grace alone, those hardships no longer haunt me, though I can understand and feel the pain of those who suffer them. This orphanage is inhabited by so many who have undergone such pain, such trauma. Amma has saved them from untold suffering and poverty. I wish to serve these people in whatever humble way I can. What greater joy can there be than in offering at Amma's sacred feet the very life that She bestowed upon me?

(April 2003)

"This kid looks like my son!"

Cecile Villacampa Toubal, Spain

During Amma's 2012 program in Penang, I went to the *Matruvani* counter to subscribe to the magazine, giving them my address in Shanghai. Having done so, I asked the staff twice, "Are you sure I will receive *Matruvani* in China?" They reassured me that I would.

And I did. I was very pleased to receive my first issue of *Matruvani* at home in Shanghai. When I saw the photo on the front cover, which featured a kid holding a yellow rose, I thought, "This kid looks like my son when he was baby!" I took a closer look at the photo. It *was* my son! The occasion came back to me. The photo was taken in Barcelona in 2006. I remember buying the yellow rose for Amma.

I thought this was amazing. It was the first time in my life that I was receiving *Matruvani*, and that, too, in China, and it had a photo of my little boy taken in Spain! What a wonderful gift from Amma! I feel that She was reassuring me that She is always with me, and that I am not alone.

~

I have been living in Shanghai since July 2010. At first, it was quite hard. The Chinese are nice people and I love them, but life here is so different from Europe that I used to feel lost all the time.

I had brought to China all my books, CDs and photos of Amma. I searched the Internet for a local Amma satsang but failed to find any.

In February 2011, my husband's brother died suddenly. My husband, son and I were very sad. This sorrow made me long for Amma even more. One evening, while praying, I started crying. "Amma, I know You are with me, but I would like to meet people who know You in Shanghai. I feel so lonely here!" I felt that I needed to share my love for Amma with other devotees. I sent emails to devotees I knew, asking them if they knew any devotee in Shanghai; they didn't. I felt very sad. I asked myself, "Why didn't I use the opportunity to learn the IAM (Integrated Amrita Meditation) technique while I was in Europe? It's too late now!"

Three days later, I received an email from a brahmacharini, who wrote that a swami from Amma's ashram would be in Shanghai in four days to conduct an IAM course. Amma had heard my prayers!

During the course, I met Lyli, a Chinese devotee from Shanghai. We organized the first satsang in my house, where the swami performed a *puja* (ritualistic worship). Just 10 days before, I would never have imagined that a swami from the ashram would come to teach the IAM technique, and be in my house, performing a puja and playing bhajans on my son's piano.

Since that day, devotees in Shanghai have been meeting every week to pray together. That's how we began an Amma family in Shanghai.

~

People sometimes ask me, "How did you meet Amma?"

My answer is, "I met Amma in a dream."

My father died in 1991 when I was 17. I loved him very much. He was a generous person, funny and always happy. For six years after his death, I worked in real estate, and felt completely cut off from everyone. I had no friends or family to help me. I decided to die. I knew that something existed after death but I didn't know what exactly. I wanted to go to my daddy.

That's when I had this 'dream.' In that 'dream,' I could embrace my father, who told me, "I don't want you to continue being so sad, thinking about me. I will show you where I am now!" He brought me to a world full of love and happiness. I cannot express in words how happy I felt there. I had never felt so happy before. I was overjoyed that I could embrace my father again. Many people in white came; they were in white not because they were wearing white clothes, but because they were garbed in white light. I couldn't understand what they said but I could feel love everywhere.

Then a woman with dark hair and brown skin arrived. She told me, "I am Amma. I will show you something." She brought me to a temple. It was square room without walls and only four columns. In the middle of the square was a pyramid of light. She told me, "This is the truth. Never forget it!" I was very happy.

After that, my father asked me to return to my world, but I didn't want to. I told him, "How can you ask me to do that? I want to stay here in this world full of love!"

He said, "You have no choice," and I had to leave.

When I woke up, I felt very elated. Everything seemed to be unusually lucid. I was in front of the sea, and I said "Thank you." I looked at the people around me and had the sensation that we were One. It was an amazing experience.

Before this 'dream,' I believed in God but had no religion. I had never read about Hinduism or Buddhism. I knew nothing about religion. During the seven years I was sad, I remembered this 'dream' and thought, "I cannot be sad. There is a world full of love."

In 2004, I was living in Barcelona with my son, who was then two months old. While going for a walk in Ciutadella Park, I found a flyer with a photo of Amma. I took the flyer and thought, "This woman looks like the woman of my dream! And it's the same name, too. How is that possible?" I read the sentences about love and peace, and had the feeling that this message come from the other world, where my father was. I took the flyer with me. I couldn't believe that it was possible for the woman of my dream to exist in my world. The flyer announced Amma's program one month later.

That year, I couldn't attend Amma's program because I had to bring my son to a doctor in France. Nevertheless, I kept the flyer with me. A year later, I attended Amma's program with my son who was then about a year old. When I saw Amma, I recognized Her immediately. I also recognized the energy or love in the space around Her, which was the same as that of the other world. When Amma says that She is in all the worlds at the same time, I know it's true.

Amma is with us every moment of our lives. She is with all those we love in this world and all the other worlds. One thing is sure: death doesn't really exist, only Love exists.

(January 2013)

Rite of
Passage

Mother of Liberty
Aswathi, U.S.A.

Life teaches us many lessons. This life has taught me a number of things. First, the Lord is the only real sustainer and the closest friend to each one. God alone knows our innermost thoughts, needs and desires, and only He can carry the burdens of our pain and suffering. Second, we bring with us baggage from our past births, and we should try not to increase that burden. Third, with real faith in God, all things are possible.

Amma is helping me to overcome many mental and physical difficulties, through which I am learning these important lessons.

I was born in Chicago, Illinois, in 1974. From what my family describes, I was a playful and interactive child, showing no signs of any major illness except eczema, an allergic skin condition. I lived in San Antonio, Texas, from the age of two to six. While here, I had severe eczema and asthma.

In 1983, while visiting India, I had severe breathing difficulty as a reaction to an Ayurvedic[1] medicine I had taken to heal my eczema. I was rushed to the hospital, and I recovered by the next day. It was my first close brush with death, and I began to understand something of the fragility of life.

....
1 Ancient Indian system of medical treatment.

When we returned from India, my family moved to New Mexico. From 1984 until May 1985, I was free from asthma and eczema. "Free at last!" I thought. But God had other plans for me...

During the Memorial Day weekend in 1985, we went to San Antonio to visit our friends. I had another severe reaction to something I ate. I went into cardio-respiratory arrest. In the house were several physicians and nurses, none of whom could revive me. We later found out that there was even a potential antidote in that house at that time, but no one remembered it. Everyone in the house became paralyzed with fear, as they saw a 10-year-old child slipping away from them. Only my mother, whose faith in God has always guided her, acted. She rushed me to the nearest hospital. This time, I took a leave of absence from this world for 87 days. The doctors didn't offer any hope. They said I was "brain dead," and suggested that I be placed in a nursing home. As my family could not imagine abandoning me, I was brought home unconscious, in a vegetative state.

Seeing me utterly helpless and unable to communicate with anyone, my family members became terribly anguished. However, they did not lose faith. They prayed that I either be released or revived, according to God's will. My mother kept a continuous vigil at my bedside, praying.

When I reflect upon the events that happened, I can see so many of Amma's teachings in practice here. We are nothing in the face of God's will. At the same time, our faith is essential in determining how we respond to destiny. Will we accept it stoically or will we try to remedy the situation? My family realized that my situation was far beyond what human hands could achieve. Their surrender helped all of us develop a deep spiritual closeness, which strengthened us for the many difficulties that would follow.

My grandmother, who could not read or write English, and had never been on an airplane before, traveled alone from Kerala to Albuquerque to support us all and offer whatever help she could. She felt so strongly that she should be there to help that she refused to wait for someone to take her to the US. While travelling, she held a sign that read "I am going to America. Please help me." She demonstrated complete surrender as well as the strength of character that comes when we have resolved to do what is right in a difficult situation.

Meanwhile, God was being flooded with calls! Prayers and offerings were being made by hundreds of relatives and friends. He decided to send me back! On August 20th, when my sister was tickling my feet, I 'woke up' from the coma with a laugh. After I regained consciousness, I would cry constantly because I didn't know what was happening to my body; it wasn't under my control any more. I was completely bedridden and could barely see. It was at this point that I truly began to experience personally the frailty of material existence. Medical doctors called my condition "anoxic encephalopathy with cerebellar damage." I call it "Amma's internal path, a spiritual passage."

We first heard about Amma in May 1987. One of my aunts had written to us about a female saint from Kerala who preached and practiced unconditional love. Luckily, we received the letter before Amma reached the US on Her first World Tour. We learned that, after California, Amma would stop next in Santa Fe, New Mexico. There is only one airport in the state of New Mexico that She could come to, and that is in Albuquerque, only 15 minutes from our house. So we did not even have to go to Her; She came to us in the deserts of New Mexico! Amma's coming brought showers of love to our parched hearts. I truly believe that the intense worship of Mother Earth by many Native Americans and others in this spiritually charged land beckoned Mother to Her children.

My family and I were amidst the handful of Western devotees who gathered to greet this 'saintly lady' from India. I was on a wheelchair and still unable to see beyond a short distance. When Amma disembarked from the plane, She walked to all of us with outstretched arms, hugged and kissed each one of us, and asked how we knew She was coming. She had the attitude of one who had known us and our past all along, and we strangely felt completely at ease with this, as if She were revisiting Her own family. We were the only family from Kerala at the airport. I held a rose in my hand for Amma, and She immediately took it, hugged my family members and me, and talked to us for a long time about our situation. She seemed not to notice even that I was physically 'different' from others. She then spoke to us in Malayalam and asked us to come to Santa Fe, where She would be staying. When we reached there, Amma talked to us for a long time and rubbed *vibhuti* (sacred ash) all over my body. I could understand what Amma was saying but I couldn't speak Malayalam fluently. Amma later asked my brother, Ashok, my sister, Asha, and me not to forget our mother tongue. We attended the evening bhajans and, after that, we were hooked! A tremendous transformation took place in each of us that I will never be able to explain. I can only say that now, it is impossible to imagine life without Amma.

We asked Amma if She would grace our house with Her physical presence. Amma came on the third day; we did not even think about performing a proper worship of Her feet, but just welcomed Her with outstretched arms and spontaneous tears. She laughed and joked with us, and then we had a small puja-and-bhajan program in the living room at home. Everyone who came had the opportunity to enjoy Amma's darshan personally. All the swamis (then young brahmacharis) shared stories of Amma with us. I remember thinking how happy and child-like they were. Most importantly, Amma's sweet smile and firm hug alleviated a lot of our sorrow. I have tried to live with this outlook, of being happy, as much as possible since then.

In 1989, we moved to Indiana and started seeing Amma in Chicago. Amma had been giving out Hershey's kisses as prasad since the early days of the US tour, when a devotee brought some of them to Her as a gift and She distributed them to all around. In 1992, in Santa Fe, during Devi Bhava, the all-knowing Amma gave me Hershey's kisses with nuts in them. Until then, we had thought that I was lethally allergic to all nuts, as that is what we think put me in a coma. Because it was prasad, I ate it right away. My prasad had nuts and my mother's did not. My mother turned around and asked me something, and when I answered, she smelled nut in my breath and panicked, but nothing happened. We felt a deep gratitude to Amma for Her protection.

Since childhood, my sister had been intending to return to India to do service there, and Amma encouraged and guided her. My brother had completely changed his life after meeting Amma. Slowly, our entire family began to shift its focus back to India. We relocated to India, and I live mostly in Amritapuri now.

In 1994, I had many physical and emotional falls. I fell into a large window and tore the dress I was wearing, but there wasn't a single cut on my body. Yet another accident occurred when I was learning to walk again. A car started unexpectedly and ran into me at low speed. Other than a few rattled nerves, I was none the worse! That same year, my allergies got worse and I became very depressed. Listening to tapes of Amma singing,

I prayed constantly, asking Her to ease my plight. She has been doing this, but in Her own way, and most often not as fast as I wished!

One year, when my family was with Amma in California, She asked me for some Indian names to give Western devotees. I gave Her long and old-fashioned Indian names like 'Parameshwaran' and 'Narayani' because I really liked them. She joked and laughed about this for a long time. Amma reminded me to laugh always, and to remember the rainbow, which makes people happy even though it is so fleeting.

In 1997, we went to Boston and Rhode Island to be with Amma. When we reached there, I had a feeling that something was going to happen, and it did! As usual, I ate the food that my mum had specially prepared for me. But I also wanted something that others were eating. My mum gave me a piece of cucumber from the salad made for the devotees. I had eaten cucumber before, but for some reason, after eating it this time, I felt extremely sick. We went to Amma for darshan, and I told Her that I wasn't feeling well. She asked me to go and lie down immediately and rest. We were on our way to our room, but my inner voice told me to lie down right where I was standing. As soon as I lay down at the entrance of the hall, I developed severe difficulty in breathing. I was immediately surrounded by my 'Amma family,' who, guided by Amma, administered the proper help. We asked Amma if I should go to the hospital, and She said yes. I was rushed to the emergency room by a devotee who knew the Boston hospitals well. By 'coincidence,' a spiritually inclined doctor who was my sister's classmate at medical school 'happened' to be on duty in that very hospital on the night I was admitted, and we were reassured by his caring and compassionate attitude. The sincerity of so many people, who are our family in Amma, was much more helpful than the medical training that was present around me in 1985 during my first arrest. I could feel in a very real way the powerful healing in Amma's presence.

I was put on a ventilator, but I was much better the next morning. I awoke feeling refreshed and renamed this ICU the 'inner care unit.' In my mind, I prayed to Amma to release me as quickly as possible from the hospital so that I could return to the hall to see Her physical form. As I felt fine that day, I was discharged in record-breaking time, just in time for the Rhode Island retreat. Everyone was amazed to see me back so fast, as if I had "just taken a short trip" (I had)! With Amma's grace, everything turned out fine.

Amma always answers the spiritual calls of Her children. If we take one step towards Her, She will take a hundred toward us. With Amma's help, I am trying to become a better person. Because I look, talk and walk 'differently,' most of my child-hood friends do not know how to relate to me, and we have grown apart. People frequently have difficulty seeing beyond my physical disabilities. They tend to either be afraid that they will hurt me, or they pity my situation. In 1998, I experienced an overwhelming bout of depression and frustration at my physical condition. Following Amma's advice, we went to Amritapuri, and my mother and I stayed there. Since then, my physical and mental health has continued getting better. I have realized that Amma sees far beyond my physical or even mental state into my heart, and She knows very well my innermost thoughts and yearnings. As a child, I could never excel in studies, like my brother and sister, because of my constant illnesses. I had always wanted to be involved in teaching in some way, so that I could express a compassionate way of teaching children and understanding their needs. Then came the coma, followed by long years of recovery that sapped my energy. It seemed that I would never be able to do anything useful in life. As mentioned earlier, Amma had advised me in 1987 to learn Malayalam. It was a simple instruction, but it affected me quite a lot. Despite my visual and motor difficulties, I learned to speak, write and read Malayalam. Knowing that my depression and frustration arose from my fear of being physically useless in life, Amma suggested that I use my knowledge of both Malayalam and English to help the foreign ashram residents learn Malayalam. I now teach a few people in the ashram, and we laugh good-naturedly at each other's mistakes. When I started doing this, I felt for the first time in my life a sense of usefulness and achievement. I know from my personal experience that this is possible only by Amma's grace.

There is a saying inscribed in the gateway to the US, at the base of the Statue of Liberty: "Bring me your tired, your poor, your huddled masses yearning to be free, and I will lift them up to the gates of heaven." Amma is the true Goddess of Liberty, for She stands silently in this ocean of samsara, Her torch of Love dispelling the darkness and hopelessness from our hearts. She is the supreme guide on our journey through and beyond this life, and Hers are the feet at which we can finally come to rest.

(April 2005)

Uplifted
Vijaykumar, India

Reminiscences can be quite painful, especially when they are built upon memories that depict oneself as a failure. Yet, I cling to these very same memories, for soon after the worst was over, they crystallized to become the greatest lessons in my life. Life dragged me through the worst, only to bring out the best in me. In the end, I became a believer.

Let me start from the beginning. The year was 1989. I was living in Kolkata and working as Managing Director of my own small, chemicals marketing firm. Business was good, and I had at my disposal all the trappings of success: a car, driver, club membership, and a contented family.

One day, my mother wrote to me from Shoranur, Kerala, about Amma, and said that I must meet Her when She went to Kolkata. In her letter, my mother also included the dates of the Kolkata programs. I could not say no to my mother, even though I was terribly reluctant to meet some woman whom others hailed as a Holy Mother. There was also the fact that most devotees were known to touch Her feet while paying salutations, a gesture that did not then find favor with my arrogant scheme of things.

Nevertheless, my wife Girija and I did go and see Amma, prompted more by curiosity than devotion. Darshan was at the Shastha Samooham Ayyappan Temple in South Kolkata. My wife and I joined the queue for darshan, and when my turn came, one of my close family friends introduced me to Amma.

To my surprise, Amma said that She had met my mother in Shoranur, where a manuscript of the commentary on the *Lalita Sahasranama* (1,000 names of the Divine Mother) written by my great grandfather, Thiruvali Vallikkat Narayana Menon, had been handed over to Her. Amma then hugged me affection-ately, overwhelming me with emotion. I immediately bowed down and touched Her sacred feet. I repeated the same gesture during every one of Amma's subsequent programs in Kolkata.

Within a year, Amma returned to Kolkata for Her second tour. This time, I was part of the organizing committee. In those days, one could spend a lot of time beside Amma. Girija and I took every opportunity to talk to Her, ask questions, and receive answers that Amma gave with humility and humor. Not long after these experiences, I began to worship Mother.

The next two years passed by quickly, though the first signs of receding profits in my business were beginning to tell on my lifestyle. The car had to be sold, and visits to the club became few and far between. One of my friends suggested that I try my hand in Ajman, in the UAE, where a Punjabi businessman involved in similar chemicals trading was looking for someone to further his interests in the region. I accepted the offer and took off.

Thus began my foray into trouble and misery. My boss in Ajman, though wealthy, was crude and rude. It was only a matter of time before the effects of his work culture began to tell on me. I was extremely lonely, thousands of miles away from my family, with no one to talk to. Being an extrovert by nature, conditions could not have been worse. Though I tried to stifle this anxiety and tension by concentrating on the business at hand, nothing seemed to be working properly. Seeking quick relief from this quagmire, I started taking anti-depressants. Soon, the drugs left an indelible stain on my personality. I became what doctors call a "nervous wreck."

During the initial years of my illness, I remember praying to Amma religiously. But as the medicine took its toll, I stopped. Six months later, I returned home to Kolkata. Having lost close to 15 kilograms, I looked gaunt and aged. Even some of my closest friends found it difficult to recognize me.

Though I had returned to the safety and warmth of my family, the appalled looks that confronted me every time I met a close acquaintance pushed me further into a shell. The result — acute depression. I tried to shut myself away from the world by not meeting anyone or even answering phone calls. Relentless visits to a local psychiatrist did little to cure my malaise. My common refrain to my wife and children, then both in their teens, was that I would very soon be on the streets.

Girija and the children countered the situation by taking care of the business that I had so dejectedly abandoned. She gained confidence by holding on to a letter Amma had written to her. When I was in Ajman, Girija had written to Amma, seeking advice and guidance to help her get through the troubled times. Amma had replied promptly, saying that She was always with her, praying for her happiness and well-being, and that no matter how bad things were, she should not forget to smile and be cheerful.

The illness lay siege for four years, by the end of which I began to develop suicidal tendencies. My wife would try to talk some reason into me and would often take me to different temples with the hope that the atmosphere there would have some effect on my mind. She made several plans to visit Amma's ashram, but somehow, they never materialized; until August 1997, that is.

On my arrival, I met Swami Amritaswarupanandaji and Swami Amritatmanandaji, both of whom had heard of my predicament. They gave similar advice: that I should talk to Amma about it.

The next morning, we went for darshan. It was a long queue, and I spent the time waiting trying to frame the conversation I wanted to have with Amma. I wanted Her to give me a solution to the problems I was facing, spelling out exactly how I should get out of the mess.

Nothing went according to my plan. The moment I stood before Amma, She delightfully exclaimed, "My son from Kolkata has finally come to see me!" She told my wife that our children had grown up. Few words, but they were enough to shatter the cocoon I had woven around myself. Hearing those words of endearment, I started weeping uncontrollably.

For four years, while I battled my mental disease, my emotions had practically dried up. I had not laughed or cried. Cynicism and sarcasm had replaced everything. And now, in this one meeting with Amma, all that changed. My emotions returned, and, within the next few hours, so did all the extrovert traits I had possessed before the medicines turned me into a zombie.

When I regained some control over my weeping, Amma hugged me again and asked me, Girija and our children to sit beside Her. She then continued receiving people and turned to me every now and then with a smile. I did not say much. The conversation I had prepared in my mind had vaporized. All that I could think about and see was Amma and Her love for me. A good two hours later, Amma got up and left. Later that evening, I met Swamiji, who asked me if I had told Amma anything about my problems. I shook my head.

The next morning, I was a changed man! My disturbed self had disappeared, and I was my normal self again. I could not believe it! My immediate reaction was to inform my wife and children. They could not believe it either. A miracle had taken place before our very eyes; a miracle, as I was to learn later, that turned my life completely on its head.

There was no telling the joy. By some miraculously, inexplicable reason, I was once again same old, garrulous person. By the time, we left Amma's ashram and returned to Shoranur, the effects of the miracle were beginning to show on everyone. Through tight embraces and delirious laughter, each of my relatives welcomed back the old Vijayan, whom they had been yearning to see for so long. Within days, I was back in Kolkata, only to repeat this joyous routine all over again with my friends there.

I had first thought of Amma as a holy woman. Now, I think of Her as an incarnation of the Goddess Herself. How She transformed my mind still remains a mystery.

Who is Amma? What makes Her so much larger than life? How does She make life's trials and tribulations easier to bear? Amma's workings remain beyond my comprehension.

Things fell into place as quickly as they had fallen apart. A month later when I heard that Amma would be coming to Chennai, I decided to go and see Her. During the darshan, I became convinced that Amma was everything that God was meant to be... and more. When I stood in front of Her, Amma's face lit up and She asked me, "Son, are you able to work properly now?" Then She hugged me tightly. This time, my emotions did not overpower my sense of speech. I told Amma that I was "absolutely back" to my usual, old self; that, in fact, I now had much more confidence than earlier and was, with Her grace and blessings, raring to face life.

A short while later, an old business associate and friend called me and asked if I was interested in setting up an organization for his company in Singapore. It was a challenging proposition. But I knew that, with Amma's grace, I could definitely deliver.

I have the firm conviction that Her grace will continue to protect my family and me, no matter what we need to endure in the future, just as it protects the multitudes who have experienced the warmth of Her hugs. May this faith never waver.

(December 2000)

A Painful Lesson
O. Sham Bhat, India

In the past, students in India regarded their teachers as Gurus. This is not a bad practice. Even one who has taught us just one letter of the alphabet has helped to reduce the darkness of our ignorance.

We regard Amma as the *Paramaguru* (Supreme Guru). She tells us that the Guru is, in fact, an embodiment of the all-pervading *shakti* (cosmic power). One who leads us to the Ultimate Truth, to God, is the Paramaguru. There is nothing impossible for a Paramaguru. She can do anything using Her enormous shakti in order to uplift the disciple who has come to seek refuge.

I have experienced Amma's infinite shakti and the flood of Her compassion.

I was born in a town called Odiyur in the district of Dakshina Kannada in Karnataka. In 1973 – '74, I was studying for the Bachelor of Arts degree at Vivekananda College in Puttoor. In those days, I was always fighting and creating trouble.

While in college, one Prof. M.S. Appa was appointed our principal. Just a few days after he joined, we had a disagreement over the college magazine, and I picked a quarrel with him. Accompanied by a group of students, I barged into the principal's office and insulted him by tearing the magazine to pieces and throwing the shreds of paper in front of him. The administrative department intervened, and the differences were settled. However, there was no doubt that my actions greatly pained the principal. It would have been no surprise if he had cursed me!

In due course, I completed my college studies, went on to study for a law degree, and eventually settled down in Mysore as a lawyer.

After some years, perhaps owing to some spiritual merit I had earned in a past life, I met Amma. The meeting took place when I was disappointed with all that life had presented me. I was sad that I wasn't getting the right compensation for the work I did. It was then that I came in touch with a *sadhak* (spiritual aspirant), who was supposed to be a psychic. He told me I was under the spell of a *guru-shaapa*, the curse of the Guru.

I was surprised! As far as I knew, I hadn't done anything so bad as to be cursed either by Amma or our ancestral Guru, the Swami of Ramachandrapura. I told the sadhak so. He replied that it need not be either of them; it could be a teacher from college, for example.

His words reminded me of that shameful episode from my college days. The sadhak smiled and said, "One of your professors cursed you!"

I was dumbfounded. This sadhak was born and raised in Mysore; he could not have known about my early life. I also became afraid of his psychic abilities. To my shock, he told me the name of the Principal, Prof. M.S. Appa! Although I was stupefied, the whole picture became clear to me.

I humbly asked him if he would suggest some remedy for the curse. He said plainly, "Go to Prof. Appa and beg his forgiveness."

I began to seek Prof. Appa's whereabouts. I learned that he was retired and had settled down in Bangalore. He had published an autobiography, in which he had recorded the incident with me, wherein I had tried to humiliate him, as the only bitter experience in all his life!

If he were still upset with me, how would I meet him? What if, seeing me, he becomes even more disturbed? What should I do?

One day, an old friend from Shimoga came to visit me. During his college days, he used to be in the company of political leaders always, but had since changed. He had become a devotee of a saint, and was leading a spiritually oriented life. As his Guru was not physically alive anymore, he wanted to see Amma so that he could ask Her about matters pertaining to his Guru. He wanted me to take him to Amma right away. "In Amma, I shall see my Guru," he exclaimed.

Amma was in Cochin then, consecrating a new Brahmasthanam temple. We traveled to Cochin. Throughout the journey, my friend narrated stories extolling the Guru's greatness. A thought crossed my mind: "Amma is a Satguru. She is the very embodiment of compassion. Would She not forgive me for my mistake with the principal?"

When I went for darshan, I prayed mentally to Amma to forgive me.

A month later, while at work, I heard a familiar voice, calling, "Sham Bhat!"

There were many clients in my office then. When I lifted my head, I saw Prof. Appa! I jumped out of my chair and greeted him reverentially. I did not know how I should talk to him.

He said that he had had a deep urge to look for me, forgive me and bless me. He had gone once to Mysore to look for me. Not finding me, he had gotten in touch with my relatives in Dakshina Kannada. With my address, he had travelled to Mysore again just to bless me!

He stayed for just a few minutes. Before leaving, he invited me to his house in Bangalore. When he reached Bangalore, he also wrote me a letter.

A few days later, I went to Prof. Appa's house in Bangalore with my wife. I earnestly pleaded with him to forgive me for my mistakes. His eyes became wet with tears. He blessed me whole-heartedly. I told him all that had happened; about the psychic who had informed me about the guru-shaapa, and my earnest prayer to Amma.

As we talked, we discovered that on the day I had gone to Cochin for Amma's darshan, Prof. Appa had been in the famous Vadukkunnaathan Temple (a Shiva temple) in Thrissur, just a few hours away from Cochin. It was there that he had felt the strong urge to find me and bless me. The feeling had been so intense that he had even purchased a gift for me. Prof. Appa presented the memento to my wife and me, thus blessing us.

I realized that if we insult anyone — a teacher or anyone else for that matter — we will reap the karmic consequence. This has become for me a lesson for life.

It was only through Amma's omnipotence that I was rid of the hell of the curse. When we bind ourselves with the love of the Mother of the Universe, all other bondages shatter.

May my experience be a lesson in humility, sincerity and loyalty to all. This is my prayer to Amma. Her compassion has no limits. The only thing we should do is bow down our heads, and the river of compassion will flood over us.

(November 2008)

New Lease on Life

Rahul Menon, India

I first met Amma when I was in fifth grade. My parents were ardent devotees and would often take me on their visits to Amma's ashram. Back then, visiting the ashram meant free-dom — from school life and the routine I was expected to follow at home — and joy, the bliss of being in Amma's arms, inhaling the sweet perfume She exuded, and receiving a candy at the end of darshan. As I grew older, I volunteered for *seva* (self-less service activities) and attended camps organized by the ashram. At home, I joined a bhajan group that sang for special occasions that devotees organized.

After college, life led me to Chennai and Mumbai. I then found a job in the sales department of a company in Dubai, UAE. I got married, and my wife and I were blessed with a child. My wife also found a job, although the remuneration was less than what we expected. Life flowed like a river that was neither slow nor turbulent.

I was not serious about my spiritual practices, although Amma figured in the background of my life. My mother, who continued going to Amritapuri regularly, would tell me about Amma, whenever we spoke.

I used to spend my weekends — which in Dubai mean Friday and Saturday — relaxing at home or going out with my wife and child. One night, after partying with friends, I was driving home when disaster struck. I must have fallen asleep while driving, the result of exhaustion and a few drinks. When I came to, I realized that I had run over a man and killed him. A few others were hurt and bruised. The act was irrevocable.

The next day, I went to the police station and surrendered, confessing my mistake. The thought that I had taken the life of a human being shocked me. The word 'remorse' does not even begin to describe how wretched I felt. I prayed to Amma for forgiveness; I also prayed that Amma takes care of his loved ones. Often, I wondered if God would ever forgive me.

The court took around three months to pronounce the verdict: ₹34 *lakhs* (₹3.4 million) blood money, ₹5 lakhs (₹500,000) fine, and two years in jail.

I had no means to pay up so much money. All I could do was pray to Amma. Until then I had thought that I did not have enough time to pray because of my busy schedule at work, but I now found myself chanting the *Lalita Sahasranama* thrice a day, praying intently, and holding on to Her feet, all day long.

I petitioned the government to reduce the fine, but nothing happened for a whole year. As an answer to my fervent prayers to Amma, my wife received a much better job offer with a good pay scale, almost at the same time that I was jailed. This ended my immediate financial worries for my wife and child.

The next great miracle took place at the end of *Ramadan*, the Islamic month of fasting. In Dubai, amnesty is granted to a few prisoners on this day, but normally only citizens benefit from this gesture. However, this time, my name was also announced with the names of others who were pardoned completely. My jail term was to be reduced, and the ₹5 lakh traffic fine was waived. However, the government could do nothing about the ₹34 lakh in damages; only the family members had the discretion to revise the sum. Though the parents of the man were sympathetic, the other family members would not relent. They insisted that I pay the entire amount.

My mother approached Amma once again and informed Her of the situation. Amma advised her to sell my newly-built house immediately and to transfer the amount quickly, because the laws of Dubai were quite strict. My mother took the necessary steps at once. She sold the house and was making arrangements to transfer the money when, wonder of wonders, an announcement came over the public address system in the jail: "You are free. You may leave now!" When I rushed out of my cabin to find out the cause of this sudden development, the authorities informed me that someone had paid the money — someone who wished to remain anonymous!

My mother again rushed to Amma and gushed, "Amma, you paid the money, didn't you?" Amma merely smiled graciously and asked her to sit near Her. Seeing the excitement, many onlookers wished to know what had happened. So here I am, telling you my story — another proof of what Amma, our beloved Guru, can do for us.

In situations of sheer desperation, we might run to the astrologer, unaware that the Guru is beyond all predictions and can change anyone's destiny by a mere resolve. Many astrologers had told my mother that I would not survive beyond 2012. Perhaps, Amma had kept me hidden in a prison cell, so that I would remain unseen by the Lord of Death!

Thank you, Amma, for this new lease on life. Make me worthy of Your grace. May my story enable others to strengthen their faith in You and move faster towards the goal of life.

(September 2014)

Transfiguration
VSK, India

Like a ship buffeted by tumultuous waves, I was totally at the mercy of the whims and fancies of my mind. I had concluded that there was no escape for me in this life. That was when Amma came into my life, lighting the lamp of love in my heart, granting me refuge, and ushering me to the shore of peace.

I had a successful career and a loving family. Sadly, I also had many vices. I was a heavy drinker and a chain smoker. I would waste my entire salary on satisfying my cravings. There were times I drank so much that my friends had to carry me home. Whenever my family members tried to persuade me to give up my bad habits, I would become infuriated and quarrel with them. At times, I regretted my actions and really wanted to get out of the vicious circle I was caught in, but I seemed to have lost all mental strength. I would fall prey to even the slightest temptation. Even de-addiction camps did not help me much.

In 1995, one of my close friends told me about Amma and how great She was. He told me to see Her when She visited Pune. I retorted, "I'm not in the least interested in Gurus or God-women." However, he kept insisting, until I finally agreed to accompany him. When I entered the ashram premises, I saw Amma sitting on the stage and singing bhajans. The atmosphere was saturated with devotion. It gave me a feeling of peace, something I had not experienced for years. Towards the end, Amma sang a bhajan that seemed to portray my own pathetic condition:

O mind, remember this supreme truth: nobody is your own!

Engaged in meaningless actions, you are whirling around in the ocean of this world...

Trapped in the subtle snare of Maya, do not forget the sacred name of the Divine Mother.

Tears filled my eyes. Nevertheless, I did not want to go for darshan. Also, I was getting restless, as I had not smoked for the last hour. I told my friend that I had "urgent work" to do and so had to leave, but he would have none of it. He forcibly made me join the darshan queue. As I approached Amma, my heart started pounding heavily. I thought, "She probably won't touch me because I am such a great sinner." But the moments that followed proved to be the turning point in my life. When my turn came, Amma took me in Her arms and said in my ear, "Naughty son, I know you are struggling. Don't worry. Amma is with you. Never lose heart!" Those words dived deep into my heart. I cried like a little baby in Amma's arms. She then asked me to sit behind Her for some time. Such love and compassion towards an insignificant one like me; I couldn't believe it! Tears continued to flow as I watched Her giving darshan to the large gathering.

After darshan, I was so filled with Amma's love that I couldn't speak. Seeing this, my friend smiled and asked, "Are you coming tomorrow?" I nodded my head fervently.

My wife and children were greatly surprised when I did not return home drunk that day, and that I was so peaceful and loving. The next day, I took my family for Amma's darshan, and after their first darshan, all of them became devotees. Slowly, I started feeling that I was regaining my mental strength, and that Amma's grace would save me. During one of the darshans, Amma whispered to me, "Son, just take one step. Amma will come down a hundred steps to uplift you. I know you are finding it difficult to abstain all of a sudden from drinking and smoking, which you have been doing regularly for so many years. Reduce it gradually, and after some time, you will gain the strength to stop completely."

I decided that I was going to try my best to conquer my weaknesses. But then a disturbing thought came to me: "Amma is here only for the next few days. Then what...?" A great fear arose within me.

"Will I fall again into the pit of darkness?" I asked Amma during the next darshan. She assured me that She would not let go of me. Amma also said that She would give me a mantra during the Devi Bhava darshan. I felt greatly relieved.

At the end of the Devi Bhava, Amma initiated me into a mantra. At that blessed moment, I felt as if all the burdens of my heart had been removed; I felt great joy and bliss. After the Devi Bhava, a brahmachari gave me instructions on the chanting of the mantra. After a few hours, Amma left for Mumbai, and I bade Her farewell with tear-filled eyes, promising Her within that I would never again stray in life and that I would chant the mantra with sincerity and devotion.

From that day onwards, I did *mantra japa* (repeated chanting of the mantra) regularly for a little time in the morning and again in the evening. Of course, controlling the wavering mind from going back to the old ways was a real fight, and there were many times when I felt I was about to drift away into the darkness again. But chanting the mantra always gave me strength and kept my mind focused on Amma. My drinking and smoking habits were greatly weakened.

A month after I received a mantra from Amma, I had reduced my drinking to one or two pegs a day. My family was pleased with the progress I was making. One day, when I sat down to pour myself a drink, the smell of alcohol suddenly seemed so nauseating to me that I could not lift the glass. It was the same brand of alcohol I had been consuming for years. From that moment onwards, I developed such an aversion to alcohol that I couldn't bear even the smell of it. Thus, with Amma's grace, my drinking came to a stop. I had reduced my smoking from three packets a day to about five cigarettes daily. Two months after I stopped drinking, I found that the smell of cigarette fumes was disgusting and would feel choked. Even when others smoked around me, I would feel as if I were suffocating. Thus, my smoking came to an end.

I had been non-vegetarian for years. I could not imagine having lunch or dinner without meat. But as the days passed, I began to feel an aversion towards non-vegetarian dishes and found the taste and smell unbearable.

In this way, Amma gradually worked on my weaknesses and removed them, one by one.

Words fall short in expressing my gratitude towards Amma, who has given my life, which was hitherto a burden to others, a purpose. I used to spend so much time in restaurants and bars, but now I spend much of my time in ashram seva and sadhana. Seeing the vast change in my life, many of my friends and colleagues have become ardent devotees of Amma. The gloom that darkened the faces of my wife and children has been replaced by broad smiles.

Amma's love and compassion have transformed countless lives. How blessed we all are to have come under the shelter of the Divine Mother, whose protection is unfailing.

(December 1997)

Welcome Back to Life
Rebekka Roininen, Finland

I always felt an emptiness and a longing for something I could not explain. Even as a child, I pondered a lot over the mysteries of life, death and eternity. I had many questions, but nobody could really explain to me what happened after death, or what eternity was, for example. I felt there had to be more to life than what I saw, but I did not know what.

My parents had learned Transcendental Meditation (TM), and they took my younger sister and me to learn it, too. We used to attend meditation retreats with them. As children, we did not appreciate TM; it seemed a little strange, as did the people! At that time, meditation, yoga and vegetarianism were considered 'weird' and foreign in our culture, and so, our parents advised us not to talk much about them to our friends, who were unlikely to understand them. Although we would have liked to be more 'normal,' we had a good and happy childhood nonetheless. I did not appreciate it at the time, but the spiritual foundation I received as a child helped me and perhaps even saved me in my later life.

As I grew up, the sense of emptiness and longing became more acute. I felt that I was always in the wrong place and that I did not belong anywhere. I was not too interested in anything, and most things in the world seemed meaningless. Education was meant for worldly success. Soft and sensitive people were not encouraged to develop the values of the heart. Because I was quiet, introverted and painfully shy, I found school and social life difficult. An intense feeling of being different from others isolated me in my own mind.

I found a medicine to cure the pain and social anxiety: alcohol. In Finland, people drink a lot, and so, it was natural to try it. Whenever I drank, I felt fearless and free. Before long, I became an alcoholic. I then started taking drugs. I traveled to and lived in different countries, trying to relieve the inner pain and emptiness, but always ruining my chances at redemption because of drugs and alcohol. I lost jobs, betrayed the trust of people, and ruined friendships. I even got arrested, causing endless worry to my family members and disappointing them.

I moved to New York City in search of a better life. But instead of improving, my life became worse. I wanted to party more and use harder drugs. I finally ended up injecting drugs. Soon, drugs became my whole life. I lived only to abuse drugs and to stay out of pain. I woke up every day with the fear of facing another day. Sometimes, I would eat from the garbage or leftovers from restaurants. Amazingly, there were always good Samaritans willing to help even people like me. This is what I learned from those days: that there are many kind people, and that I was always being protected.

I tried to get rid of my addiction many times but failed. I went to detoxification clinics, but would start abusing drugs as soon as I came out. I was convinced that there was no way out, that I was crazy, and that I was going to be like this for the rest of my life, which I did not think would last much longer.

I decided that I had had enough. After trying for a week to get admitted, I was finally admitted into a long-term hospital detoxification program, and somehow managed to stay there. The first week or two, I could not sleep or eat, and for another couple of weeks, I kept vomiting whatever I ate. I was afraid to talk to people. I forced myself to stay and bear it because I did not want to go back to my old life again. It took almost inhuman strength to have faith in and stay with the recovery program, to face myself, and to try and change everything about myself and my life.

The recovery program was marvelous. It accepted people who had no other refuge. There were criminals, prostitutes and vagabonds. I knew people who had killed for drugs. They had never had the same chances in life that I had received. The program's slogan was 'Welcome back to life!'

The program promoted a strict discipline and many spiritual ideals. There, for the first time, I felt that people liked me for what I was and that they believed in me. For the first time, too, I felt that I had friends. I saw that even the most desperate and hardened human beings had some goodness in their heart. They were so generous that I feel I owe my life to them.

My mother and sister traveled all the way to that dangerous neighborhood in New York to see me. It was painful to face them but they were very supportive. My mother only asked, "How can we help?" My parents never lost hope in me. My mother told me she had seen an "Indian holy mother," "Amma," and gave me a *mala* (rosary) She had blessed. I accepted it right away. Later, my mother told me that she had dreamt that Amma hugged me, before she even met Her.

Soon after this meeting, something changed. I remember telling my counselor this, and he asked me what I thought it was. I still remember my exact answer: "I have peace of mind." Somehow, the addiction no longer had the same hold on me anymore. My life changed. I left drugs and alcohol, and never went back to my old ways.

I returned to Europe and started meditating again. I knew that spirituality was the only lasting answer to anything. It was the only way to survive in life. My mother called me to say that Amma was visiting, and that I could go and see Her. I felt joy and excitement, and instantly felt that I wanted to meet Amma. I remember boarding a bus on a dark, rainy autumn night. When I arrived at the hall, even at the door, I felt something special. I received Amma's darshan and sat at the back of the hall, not fully understanding everything. It was hard to believe that there was someone like Amma, someone who could unconditionally love and accept everyone. It was something I could never have imagined until I met Amma.

The first meeting was not dramatic. I did not feel then that my life had profoundly changed, but something stayed with me. I put Amma's photo on the wall and would look at Her smiling face sometimes, but did not think much about it until the next year, when I felt that I had to see Her.

Meanwhile, my outlook on life started to change. I had always thought about the mysteries of life, but now I really wanted to find an answer, and I felt that the intellect could not provide one. I started longing for a more spiritual life. This was confusing because I now had a new life that I wanted to make full use of — to study, to forge a career, and to live a comfortable and 'normal' life. In other words, I wanted to do what I could not do before. Instead, I started thinking more about Amma and the spiritual life. Nothing the world had to offer seemed satisfying enough or worth the struggle. In any case, I had already tried looking for happiness outside, with disastrous results!

Slowly, Amma's presence permeated my life, and after coming to India, I knew there was no other choice but to stay with Her. I wanted to dedicate my life to my spiritual ideal.

Once, I asked Amma why I had to suffer from drug addiction. I had to know why someone like me, who had all the chances in life, ended up like this. She looked at me very lovingly and touched my arm. I can still see the look and feel that touch. She told me that I had to experience the negative side of life so that I would never again return to it. I had to accept what had happened and leave it behind. That was the final healing touch. I really believe that since then, I have become free. I have never since felt like using drugs. Amma not only saved me and my family from my addiction, She gave me so much more: the highest ideal to follow, the life of true love and humanity.

Before I met Amma, I had led the most undisciplined and chaotic life. Following spiritual disciples has not been easy, but Amma has encouraged me to do whatever I can. She does not force us to do anything or accept anything when we are not ready to do so. My experience is that She always focuses on the positive in us, and I feel that She wants us to do it, too. She gives us suggestions but I think that She really wants us to make the choice. She knows that we have to be ready, and if we are not, She will patiently wait until we have the maturity to receive what She wants to give. I do not think of myself as a great sadhak, and I do not feel that I am especially skilled or talented in anything. I cannot even sit straight for meditation! But I can do what I can to better myself. I owe it to the world, to my parents, and to all the people who helped me to make the best of myself. Even if I sometimes feel like a failure, I think, "At least, I'm trying to improve myself. I'm not like I was before." Having lived the inhuman, loveless life of selfishness and negativity, I can only improve. Having had my life restored to me as a gift, I feel that it does not even belong to me. I have a debt to repay the world.

Amma does not expect anything from us, not even our love. I once told Her that I did not know if I loved Her. She answered, "Don't worry about whether you love Amma or not. Amma loves you. Love your Self." If we cannot be open to divine love, how can we ever give from our limited store of love?

Sometimes, I look back and wonder how I ended up in Amma's ashram. What divine grace saved me and gave me this life, so full of beauty, love and fulfillment? I still do not know how it happened and I still cannot understand it. I know that many people cannot rid themselves of their addictions. I am grateful and want to live the life that was given back to me in the best way I can, and if possible, in some small way, try to help and bring happiness to others.

Some of us have to suffer intensely so that we can turn to God. Suffering also brings a gift: a deeper understanding of life, humility, gratitude and, most of all, an understanding of others' sufferings. Maybe, my experience can inspire or help someone. May Amma bless us all with a kind and loving heart.

(October 2014)

That Cigarette Stub
Indira, India

In some houses, one can see vases with beautiful albeit artificial flowers that may even exude a fragrance. But no bee ever comes to these flowers because they do not pulsate with life.

For many, spirituality is like those artificial flowers. It used to be no different in my case. In the morning, I would be chauffeured to important temples nearby. The chief priest himself would come immediately to welcome me and give me prasad. I would give him a generous *dakshina* (honorarium) and also donate generously to the temple. If ever I attended a spiritual discourse, I would make sure that I was seated in the front row with the important guests. In short, my husband and I were among the well-known 'spiritual' people in the city. As far as my husband was concerned, making donations was a respectable way of spending unaccountable income.

Isn't it common to buy insurance policies for everything? My husband and I decided that we would buy an insurance policy on God's grace, too. Our premium took the form of *homas* and *pujas* (forms of ritual worship) that we conducted regularly in our home. Many friends and relatives would attend these pujas. On these occasions, my husband never felt guilty about having a drink with his close friends. He would also smoke, using the cigarette he was smoking to light his next one. The only time one could see him without cigarette smoke issuing from his mouth was when he ate or slept or while he was in a temple.

Today, all that seems like a bad dream. Our old friends now say, "Oh, Indira! She was such a devout lady. Everything changed after she met Sri Mata Amritanandamayi Devi. Nowadays, she walks around like a widow, wearing white clothes. What a shame!"

I cannot blame them for their misunderstanding. They can no longer party in our house in the name of pujas. They cannot use our car to visit distant temples and other spiritually less uplifting places because we don't own a car anymore. The donations we used to make for arranging dances and dramas during temple festivals have become nominal.

In the beginning, when we heard that Amma was visiting the city we were living in, we ignored the news completely because no one had invited us to lead the welcome committee. But when we saw Amma attracting astonishingly huge crowds, we decided to go, thinking that we had nothing to lose but might gain something.

When we went to see Amma, we carried fruits, clothes, dakshina, etc. on a large plate. Replying formally to the humble greetings of the organizers and brahmacharis, we took our place among the important guests waiting for Amma's special darshan.

"What time will we be able to see Amma?" we asked.

"Hard to say. Swamiji has informed Amma. She will call you," we were told.

When we became tired of waiting, we thought, "Is there no proper protocol here for receiving important guests? Hasn't Amma been informed about who has come to see her?"

Soon, a brahmachari came running. "*Om namah shivaya!* Amma's calling you."

I am unable to say anything about our first meeting with Amma. Lines from a bhajan come to mind:

kannangu poka manavum calikka

vaakkangu mookam nin munnilamme

The eyes cannot reach You. The mind cannot grasp You.

Words become hushed in Your presence.

Amma laughed heartily at our offering. "Son, this isn't what Amma wants."

"Just tell me what Amma wants, and I will bring it," responded my husband.

As he said this, the thought that went through my mind was how much money Amma would ask for the temple fund.

"Son, when you come the next time, bring a box of cigarettes for Amma. You don't have to bring good cigarettes. Just bring the stubs you throw away after smoking. Will you bring them for me?"

In my husband's face, I saw the look of a child whose mother has caught him smoking. By the time we reached the car, his attitude had changed.

"Why limit myself to just one carton of cigarette stubs? I'll give Her a suitcase full of them. We must never give too little." Laughing bitterly, my husband said, "Joke of the year!"

As soon as he got into the car, my husband lit a cigarette. But where was the enthusiasm he usually showed in lighting up? He took one or two puffs with a look that suggested he was drinking castor oil! Throughout the journey home, the cigarette stayed in his hands. He dropped it when it was about to burn his fingers. When I got out of the car, I picked up that stub and put it in an empty cigarette carton, saying, "One!"

Neither of us ate supper. We were devouring all the books we had bought, shedding tears as we read. We slept late at night, not in our air-conditioned bedroom but on the carpet in our veranda. Our children, who decided that their parents had gone crazy, no longer say that, because Amma has since become their Father, Mother, Guru and God.

During our next darshan, i.e. the next morning, we alighted from the bus along with our children and waited patiently in the long queue for our turn, holding the only thing we had to offer at Amma's feet — a cigarette carton with just one stub!

(July 2016)

Anointment

Divine Grace
MKR, India

I first saw Amma in March 1998. Though I believed in God, I harbored the foolish delusion that it was important to earn money first and to acquire a prominent status in society; then, after one has turned 60, one could begin doing spiritual practices, when retiring from active social life!

I had a business that supplied chemicals. I had many orders in hand, and was happily sailing along. I was very proud of my achievements, which I thought were due solely to my adept managerial skills. I considered myself a man of immense mental strength and great optimism. But I was soon to realize that the notions I had about myself were completely wrong.

In June 1997, my life took a drastic turn. My competitors spread false propaganda about the products we supplied, and the clients believed them. As a result, the delivery of large stocks of chemicals was blocked, leading to the loss of a great amount of money. Although I tried my best to find new openings, all my efforts were in vain. I had to redeem my debts and pay my employees their salary, but there was no income. During this financial crisis, I spent many sleepless nights, brooding over my fate. My son had just finished his 12th grade at school and wanted to pursue a degree in engineering, but I didn't have enough money even to pay for his admission. To add to my woes, my wife became terribly sick and had to be hospitalized. Soon my suppliers, whom I owed money, filed legal notices against me. All these blows were too much for me to bear. I could see no hope in the future. Who could pull me out from the ocean of misery I was in?

I began to contemplate suicide, but even as I made preparations to do so, the thought of my wife and children would come to mind, preventing me from taking any drastic step. It was at this time that I learned about Amma through a relative who visited my wife in the hospital. He was an ardent devotee of Amma and would often visit Her. He gave me hope, saying that I should have faith in Amma, who is the Divine Mother incarnate, and the embodiment of love and compassion. He gave me the dates of Amma's visit to Mumbai, and also gave me an audio tape of Amma's bhajans. When I heard Her voice, I couldn't control my tears. I felt a great peace filling my heart, and felt that the burden of sorrows had been reduced to a great extent. I resolved to meet Amma.

I arrived at the Mumbai ashram on the first day of the Brahmasthanam temple festival. There was a huge gathering of people, and I felt doubtful that I could meet Amma and tell Her my problems. One of the brahmacharis whom I met assured me that Amma would meet each and every person. As I stood in line for darshan, there were doubts in my mind. I thought, "Amma is said to be omniscient and omnipotent. Does She know my problems?" As I came closer to Amma and saw Her compassionate, smiling face, I started to cry. When it was my turn for darshan, I just broke down in Her arms. Amma said in my ears, "Darling son, the Divine will take care of everything. Give this apple to your wife in the hospital." She placed prasad and an apple in my hands. I had not said anything about my problems. How did Amma know that my wife was in the hospital? As I came out of the hall, I was a different man. I knew Amma would take care of me.

From the ashram, I went straight to the hospital, and gave Amma's prasad to my wife. She had become very weak and frail, owing to her illness. The doctors were unable to diagnose her illness.

That night, I slept soundly for the first time in many months. When I visited the hospital the following afternoon, the doctors informed me that my wife's temperature, which had been very high for several days, had normalized. Even the blood tests conducted in the morning revealed that everything was fine. The doctors were surprised. I told them that my wife's recovery was the result of the unique blessings of Amma, the divine physician. My wife and I shed tears of gratitude to Amma.

From the hospital, I went straight to see Amma. When I told Her that She had cured my wife, Amma laughed and said, "Divine grace saved her."

I replied, "I know who the Divine is: Amma!"

During the next two days, I spent most of my time in the ashram, and by the last day, I felt a great transformation taking place in me. During Devi Bhava darshan, I received a mantra from Amma, who left for Baroda the next morning. Bidding farewell to Amma was really heartbreaking for me.

As the days went by, I started chanting my mantra regularly, and whenever I found time, I visited the ashram. My wife was discharged from the hospital. Although my financial condition had not improved, I felt a great inner strength to face the situation.

One day, I received a legal notice informing me that I would have to deposit a large amount of money within a week, or face legal action. I tried my best to raise the amount, but no one was ready to help me. Three days before I was due to make the payment, I cried before Amma's photo, praying to Her to show me a way out of this crisis. The following afternoon, I received an envelope by courier. It was from one of my old clients, expressing regret for cancelling an earlier order of chemicals because of false propaganda spread by my competitors; this client also wanted to resume dealings with my company, and had enclosed a check as an advance. The amount was exactly what I had to deposit in two days' time. Placing the envelope in front of Amma's photo, I prostrated before Her, tears flowing down my cheeks.

Today, the situation has totally changed. Most of my clients have returned, and I have almost redeemed all my debts. By Amma's grace, my son was accepted into the engineering course. All my family members have become ardent devotees of Amma. Without fail, we sit together every day to do *archana* (chanting of a litany of divine names) and to sing bhajans. And whenever we get a break, even if it is only for a week, we rush to Amritapuri for Amma's darshan.

(February 1999)

True Payasam
Ahalya (Maila Korhonen), Finland

I first heard about Amma in the spring of 1995 through a documentary on Finnish TV. That short program was enough for me to realize that She was my only hope to understand the real purpose of life.

Previously, I had tried to find meaning in life by fighting revolutionaries in order to reduce the suffering of the poor.[1] I believed that material well-being would solve their problems. One can offer one's whole life to help the poor, but even a thousand lives are not enough, if the meaning and goal of life are not understood. After many years, I had come to realize that nothing had really changed; nothing except my hope — I had lost it.

After seeing Amma on TV, the hope that I could gain an understanding of the meaning and goal of life was rekindled. I tracked down the producer of the documentary and bought a copy of the video so that I could see more of Amma. In the months that followed, She was constantly on my mind. I even dreamt of Her. Finally, I knew I had to find a way to see Her. I had heard that She was coming to Stockholm in August. I did

---

1 The civil war in El Salvador between 1980 and 1992.

not have the money to travel there, but somehow I managed to find it.

The days in Stockholm with Amma were unforgettable. I had the feeling that I had already been with Her, and that I would soon be with Her again. I also felt this closeness with Her ashram children. I began to wonder how to get to India. I knew it would take time, and so decided that I would learn Malayalam, Amma's mother tongue, to prepare myself. But how to learn Malayalam in Finland?

Sitting in front of Her picture, I spoke to Amma: "I would like to speak Your language. One day, I will speak to You in Malayalam." I also told one of Amma's daughters in Finland about my desire, and she offered me a book that teaches Malayalam. On returning home, I ran to Amma's picture to thank Her. When I opened the book, I discovered that it explained Malayalam in English, not in Finnish. I began to search everywhere for someone to teach me Malayalam. Only a few people in Finland are from India; to find someone from Kerala seemed almost impossible.

I prayed to Amma again and again. One Friday evening, I called the Indian embassy, but it was closed. Now, even that slim hope had to wait until the next week. The next day, I went to a photo shop to make a copy of a picture of Amma. The man behind the desk told me to leave the photo on the table and return in 30 minutes. When I was about to leave, the shopkeeper looked at the photo and said that perhaps he could make the copy in a couple of minutes.

There were not many customers in the shop, and most were lined up at the other desk. Looking behind me, I saw a couple with a small child. They had not been there a moment before. They smiled at me brightly. I returned their smile. They seemed familiar to me, and looked as if they were from India. The woman came up to me and asked if the woman in the picture was from India. I said, "Yes, actually She is from Kerala. She is a Holy Mother."

"I'm from Kerala, too," she said.

"How nice! I'd like to learn Malayalam," I said immediately.

"I can teach you," she answered. Everything happened so fast and without any obstacles.

The woman's motivation was not money, which was fortunate for me, for I had little. She was keen to teach not only me, but Amma's other Finnish children as well. The woman did not know Amma. Now She does, and now I am learning Malayalam. We both feel that Amma brought us together. Bringing me and one of the few people in Finland who speaks Malayalam together in the same place and at the same time can only be the work of God.

~

Often, I have wondered about the source of the sweetness that attracts us to Amma. The only other place where I have tasted so much sweetness is the *Puranas,*[2] especially the stories of Lord Krishna. Slowly, after observing Amma, I began to understand the reason for that sweetness. Amma's every action and word, everything about Her, is sweet because of Her purity, love, selflessness and detachment. She expresses everything fully and perfectly. I once saw Her picking up a tiny insect from Her lap with a stick, and then letting it down on the floor, with total concentration, patience and carefulness. In that single gesture, I felt the sweetness of Her love towards each and every being in creation. Just as sugar has properties to conserve food, Amma's sweetness conserves memories of experiences with Her in our hearts so that we can enjoy them and reflect on them again and again, and thus imbibe their true meaning.

The following experience showed me that Amma is the real doer and that She is all-pervading. It took place in Amritapuri a few days before my birthday some years ago. At that time, Amma was in North America. On that day, while sitting in the meditation hall, I mentally told Amma that it would be nice if

---

2 'Ancient (lore).' Hindu scriptures containing ethical and cosmological teachings relative to Gods, man and the world. They revolve around five subjects: primary creation, secondary creation, genealogy, cycles of time and history. There are 18 major Puranas.

there could be *payasam* (sweet pudding) for all the ashram residents on my birthday. Usually, we get payasam only when someone donates a sum of money with the specific request to use it to treat ashram residents to payasam. In my prayer, I mentioned to Amma that I wouldn't mind not getting it. I then forgot all about it.

On my birthday, I did not go for lunch. I spent that time instead with some friends from Finland. We ate fruits and sang bhajans, then went for a swim. At the swimming pool, I asked another resident what she had had for lunch. She gave a strange reply: she had gone for lunch but didn't know what had been served. When I asked her to explain herself, she said that she had gone to the dining hall only to take the payasam that was being served there.

I went to the kitchen immediately and asked if there was payasam for lunch. One of those working in the kitchen told me that there had been, but that there was no more left. I told her that I just wanted to know who had sponsored it. One brahm-acharini told me that an elderly man staying in the ashram had sponsored it for all the ashram residents to mark his birthday, even though it was not his birthday that day. He was ailing and staying in the ashram hospital; he wanted to treat all the ashram residents in case he did not live to see his next birthday.

When I heard this, I went to the hospital to see this person. When I told him about my prayer for payasam, he was delighted. Though it wasn't his birthday, he had, in a way, celebrated it by giving the ashram residents a treat. We both felt blessed to have become Amma's instruments in this sweet event. A few months later, he passed away. In those months, that was the only time we had payasam.

The way in which Amma orchestrated this whole episode reminded me of the saying that God does everything without doing anything. Amma makes us act. This experience also showed me that though we may not realize it, we are instruments in God's hands.

Of course, someone who doubts Amma's divinity could well ask, "How do you know it was Amma who answered your prayer? Maybe it was God who answered your prayer!" I would tell him or her the following experience that gives me the faith that God and Amma are one and the same.

One night, many years ago, I was sitting on my bed in a room facing the back yard of the building where Amma stays. It was midnight. Amma was sitting on a stool under a tree; a few swamis and brahmacharis were sitting around Her. I was reflecting on my stay in the ashram. At that time, I had been staying there for two-and-a-half years. I had no more money left. A deep sadness filled my heart. I didn't know what to do. I did not yet have enough faith in Amma, and therefore fell into a state of desperation.

In that mood of sadness, I began to pray to God — not to Amma. In those days, before I had developed faith in Amma's divinity, I would call out to God — God without a specific name, form or quality. I asked Him to guide me: "Dear God, tell me what I should do? Where should I go if I am not meant to stay here? I want to dedicate my life to You." The prayer came from the bottom of my heart. I really wanted to know what God's will was regarding my life. After the prayer, I saw through the window that Amma was still sitting on the stool, surrounded by the swamis and brahmacharis. I wondered if Amma was aware that I had directed my prayers to God and not Her.

The very next day, someone told me that Amma was calling me. But by the time I received the message, darshan was already over and Amma had returned to Her room. The next darshan day, I went to Amma. Calling me by my name, She looked into the eyes, making me feel very close to Her. She then said, "You stay!" And then She continued giving darshan as usual. Was that all, I asked myself, a little confused? But that, indeed, was all; Her answer said everything. I had not told anyone about my prayer. Only 'God' knew my exact question. And Amma had responded directly to my questions to God.

Amma says that such is the power of a *mahatma's* (spiritually illumined soul's) words that they become true sooner or later. My problem was resolved and I am still staying in Amritapuri.

I have had other similar experiences of Amma's omniscience. They have made me realize that She is, in reality, the all-knowing one. We are just not aware of Amma's role in everything. We are so caught up with our mental chatter that we fail to hear the gentle, voice of Amma within. Once, I prayed to Amma before sleeping, asking Her why I could not see Her, that is, the real Amma, not just Her physical manifestation. During my sleep, She appeared in the form of Balagopal, the child Krishna, and revealed Herself through the eyes and smile. Amma then came from somewhere else, interrupting the dream that I was seeing at that moment, and said, "Because you are always engaged with so many things." She didn't make any introductory remark like, "*Om namah shivaya*. Regarding your question last night, here is the reply." She just said, "Because you are always engaged with so many things." She then disappeared. After contemplating on that sudden visit and Her direct reply, I had no doubt that this statement would not have come from someone who isn't aware of my thoughts and watching over me all the time, even in my dreams.

Experiences like these do not just make one aware of Amma's omnipresence and omniscience. She is not interested in showing us how great She is; for Amma, there is no 'I' and 'you,' only the Supreme Self or Pure Consciousness or whatever we may call it. Amma is interested only in helping us progress in our path towards that realization. Through an awareness of Amma's constant presence, we become more aware and alert about our thoughts, words and deeds. We are used to thinking that no one knows what we do when we are alone or what we think. But once we become really aware and not just superficially, once we get tangible experiences that Amma is omnipresent, and that not even one thought can rise in our minds without Her knowing it, we will inevitably come down from our throne of 'I' and 'mine' and bow down humbly at Her sacred feet and, with cupped and empty hands, wait patiently for the true payasam that She wants to offer us, the nectar of immortality. May that day come to us soon!

(March 1997)

Magic Touch

Andrew Bukraba, Australia

It was a Saturday evening in January 1994. The weather along the sandy coast of the Arabian Sea in Kerala, South India, was warm and humid, but a gentle and cooling sea breeze gave some relief. From time to time, the bluish lights of gigantic fireflies would illuminate the darkness under the coconut palms. It looked as if they were trying to reach the stars that filled the Indian sky. The ashram atmosphere was saturated with Amma's presence, Her divine energy. She was distributing prasad in the meditation hut to all the ashram residents. A long queue of people emerged from the darkness and disappeared into the light framed by the doorway of the small thatched hut. All were silent and seemed to be contemplating the special privilege of being fed by the Incarnation of Love, beloved Amma.

Near the meditation hut stood a visitor, hidden in the shadows cast by a dense bush. Hailing from Australia, he had arrived just a few days before. He had never visited India or the ashram before, but from the very first moment, he felt at home. That afternoon, he had learned from others that Amma distributes prasad on Saturdays evenings to ashram residents who fast on that day. He realized that he could not join the others to receive the prasad as he was neither an ashram resident nor had he fasted that day. His emotional state was such that this seemed like an almost unbearable tragedy. He experienced a strong conflict between his identification with ashram life and his status as a visitor. This resulting agony manifested as an uncontrollable stream of tears and a temporary loss of interest in everything around him.

After a while, the distribution of prasad ended, and he heard the chanting of the 15th chapter of the *Bhagavad Gita*. Although he did not understand the Sanskrit verses, they nevertheless sounded familiar, and brought a slight relief to his sufferings. Somehow, the chanting had a calming effect on his nerves. It sounded like an echo of something forgotten long ago.

The ashram residents started leaving the meditation hut. Suddenly, one of the Western residents, whom the visitor knew from Amma's Australian tours, walked to the very spot where he was hiding. Somehow, not looking surprised at seeing a dark figure under the bush, she sat down as if it were the most normal thing to do, and asked, "Please, won't you take some of my prasad? We can share it, can't we?"

The visitor readily took some of it in his hand. He was so surprised that he could hardly manage to say, "Thank you." The sweetness of the prasad was unbelievable! It was like heavenly nectar. He felt as if it had come straight from Amma's hand. All of it was so amazing and unexpected, like the final act of a drama directed by some invisible playwright.

But it was not the final act. A few minutes later, he noticed some movement among the ashram residents standing at the entrance to the meditation hut. Amma was coming out! The visitor sank deeper into the shadows of the bush. He did not want to be in Amma's way or to be noticed by Her in his present misery. To his astonishment, Amma walked straight towards him. He was exhausted after his long cry and stunned by Her approach. He was not even able to prostrate. He just stood there, motionless, feeling like an utter idiot. Amma gently touched his chest and rubbed his right arm in a deft motion. She did not stop or say anything as She passed him on Her way to the grove of young mango trees. He could not see Amma's facial expression because of the darkness, but he felt that She was smiling lovingly and with full understanding of his mental state.

His reaction to this magic touch was instantaneous. His feeling of being shipwrecked, unwanted, unrecognized and useless vanished immediately. A feeling of love germinated in his heart; it was the bliss of happiness and gratitude for Amma's all-knowing compassion and for the miracle of the instant healing of his bleeding heart.

Now calm, he meditated for a long time under the coconut palms. The mighty waves of the nearby sea beat the sands of the shore, implanting into his subconscious the truth about his destiny: "Om... you belong here. Om... be patient. Om...

everything takes place according to the divine will. Om... Amma is always with you. Om... Om... Om..."

At the beginning of December 1995, a new ashram resident was standing in a long queue to receive Amma's Saturday prasad for the first time. He was concentrating deeply on every detail of this new experience. This was the same man who had once stood crying under a dense bush in the darkness of the night, close to the meditation hut where Amma was giving prasad. Now his turn had come. He knelt in front of Amma with great respect. She quickly put prasad on his plate and looked straight into his eyes. She did not say a word and only smiled lovingly, but he understood the language of the silence: "You see, all is well. I told you, you belong here. Now, concentrate on the present. Do not think about the past or imagine the future. Do your sadhana. Do not worry about anything. I will take care of you. I am with you always."

One loop of time had closed. One battle in his struggle for Freedom had been won. There will be more battles to fight, but now he is aware that he is not on his own. Amma is walking the path with him, step by step.

(December 1996)

Mysterious Messenger

Satish Kumar V., India

The thread asked the candle
why u dissolve urself when I burn.
The candle said
When those who r in my heart suffer
I am bound to shed tears.

On the evening of December 15th, 2005, I was feverish and had severe body pain. I couldn't even walk. I consulted the campus doctor, who told me that it could be the beginning of a viral fever, and gave me some medicine. I took the first dose and went to bed. The body pain was so excruciating that even lying down didn't alleviate the pain. I started crying and called out, "Amma! Amriteshwari!" Gradually, a feeling of utter uselessness began to overwhelm me. In sheer frustration, I started shouting at Amma. "Amma, what difference will this sinner make if he remains alive? I don't want to live to see the next morning." I went on pleading with Amma to release me from life, until I slipped into a deep sleep.

The next morning, contrary to expectation, the body pain had abated somewhat, and I was able to walk around. I took a refreshing hot-water bath. While getting ready for the day, I received an SMS (Short Message Service). The message read,

"The thread asked the candle why u dissolve urself when I burn. The candle said When those who r in my heart suffer I am bound to shed tears... Gud Mrng!"

I liked the philosophical flavor of the message. I couldn't identify the sender by the number. However, I replied with an SMS: "Good morning and thank you for your message."

In the afternoon, after lunch, I received another SMS while climbing the stairs to my room. The message read, "LIFE never seems to be the way we want it, but we LIVE it the best way we can. There is no PERFECT life, but we can fill it with PERFECT MOMENTS... Gud aftrnun!"

I was astonished to see such a philosophical message again, and I replied "Good afternoon, and thank you for your kind message. May I know the identity of the sender?"

I received a reply soon, "Aren't u Sati?... If not, me seriously sorry 4 d disturbance." I was stunned. Only the elders in my home call me 'Sati.'

As the sender had not revealed his/her identity, I decided to call the number. A woman answered the call. I identified myself and asked her how she knew me. She said, "Are you not the one who fought with me last night?" She spoke English with a foreign accent. What she said didn't make any sense. For one thing, I had been bedridden the night before. For another, I had spent that time haranguing Amma until I slept. I asked the woman how she had obtained my number. She replied that her friend had my number. This answer made me more even more perplexed. I told her I hadn't fought with anyone the night before. The woman apologized for disturbing me and said goodbye.

I wanted to get in touch with this woman again and to find out more about her. I sent her an SMS: "I like the philosophical messages you sent me. What about starting a friendship based on such philosophical exchanges? Hope we can." But I didn't receive any response. I tried to call the number several times but always received the same message: "The number you have called is switched off. Please call again later." After some time, I stopped calling.

The next morning, while chanting the *Lalita Sahasranama*, a question crept into my mind: "Weren't you fighting with Amma on the night of December 15th? You were shouting at Her, begging Her to relieve you of your misery!" It gradually dawned upon me that the messages that I received on December 16th were nothing but responses to my confused state of my mind and answers to the questions I had been hurling at Amma. The use of my pet name 'Sati,' a personal detail, and the reference to the angry exchange I had with Amma on the night of December 15th reinforced this belief.

Thereafter, I called the unidentified number many times. Every time I called, I would expect to hear the same message: "The number you have called is switched off. Please call again later." And I did until one day, I got another message: "The number you called does not exist." Thereafter, I kept getting this message whenever I called that number.

I couldn't help feeling convinced that the caller and sender of those philosophical messages had been none other than Amma. I saved the number in my cell phone against the name 'Vallickavu Amma.'[1]

(June 2006)

---

1 Amma is known among some devotees as Vallickavu Amma as Her ashram is in Vallickavu.

All-knowing Mother
Amit Kadam, India

Amma has blessed me with many experiences. Let me share just a few experiences that I had when I visited Amma's ashram at the end of 2005.

My mother and I were scheduled to leave home on December 22nd and return on December 27th. My wife, who was pregnant, was due to deliver around January 14th.

December 10th: My wife had her third ultrasonography. The reports showed that there was a lot of water surrounding the fetus and that its head was much bigger than it should have been. My wife was in her 32nd week of pregnancy, and the size of the fetus's head was that of a 38-week-old fetus. The doctor said that the baby might be born prematurely, some time between December 22nd and 24th. He said that my wife would need to undergo another ultrasonography around December 19th in order to determine the date of the Caesarian section. This meant that I would have to cancel my trip to Amritapuri. Just before cancelling my booking, I placed my hand on my wife's stomach and prayed to Amma, "If You really listen to Your devotees, You will solve this problem and call me to You." I consoled my wife, and told her that everything would be fine, by Amma's grace.

December 19th: The ultrasonography report showed that the size of the fetus's head hadn't changed and that the water level was coming down. The miracles had started! We took the report to the doctor, who said that he would not operate on her but wait until the 27th (the date I was scheduled to return from Amritapuri). He said he would check my wife on the 26th to see if he could perform the Caesarian on the 27th. Amma had paved the way for my visit!

December 25th, Amritapuri: We heard that Amma had returned at around 2 a.m. from Her visit to Chennai. I was excited. Earlier, I had already decided that I wouldn't eat anything until Amma gave me darshan. I started doing seva in the kitchen, cooking food and helping in any way I could. My mum told me that people were saying Amma would not be giving darshan, and that there was no point fasting. But I was determined to stick to my resolution.

As the day passed, I worked hard in the kitchen. While working, I prayed to Amma, "You are the omniscient divine power. You can give me darshan if You want. I have come from so far away. Please don't let me go just like this. My return flight is on the 27th and I had heard that You would give darshan on the 27th. Please give me Your darshan."

I then learnt that reporters from news agencies such as BBC Radio had come to interview Amma. I was a little disappointed, thinking that my last chance to get Amma's darshan was gone. The reporters came into the kitchen to interview those working there, and I thought I would also be interviewed. But it was not to be. They interviewed one person and left. I waited outside the kitchen for some time so that I would get a glimpse of Amma's blissful form if She came down. While waiting there, I felt I should change my shirt. It had been white, but food stains had since soiled it. I left for my room to change into a clean shirt. When I returned, I learnt that the reporters had been called into Amma's room. I felt so despondent thinking that I hadn't had the good fortune of getting Amma's darshan.

While talking to the security guards about the good fortune of the reporters, one of the reporters came down from Amma's room and asked for chairs. I quickly grabbed two chairs, told the security guard that I was taking the chairs upstairs to Amma's room. The door was open — Amma was sitting in a chair. I was so pleased to see Her. That one glimpse of Amma was enough for me! That was the darshan I had been longing for. But there was more to come. Someone inside Amma's room told me to leave the chairs outside and to come and sit inside. I stepped inside and someone closed the door. I couldn't believe it! Here I was, sitting in Amma's room, so close to Her and staring at Her captivating form. Tears started rolling down my cheeks. I wanted to kiss Her feet, but I controlled myself. For the next hour or two, I sat gazing at Amma, totally oblivious to what the reporters were asking Her or what was happening around me. I was in a state of indescribable bliss!

When the interview ended, Amma offered prasad to everyone. I wanted to get the prasad from Amma's hand, too, but I was too scared to ask for it. What if Amma asked who I was? What answer would I have? I was neither a reporter nor a brahmachari. At that point, Amma looked at me and offered me the prasad. I couldn't control myself any longer. I just fell at Her feet and started crying. I kissed those sacred feet and remained in that position for a minute. Amma waited for me to get up. She then hugged me and asked why I was crying. I explained to Amma and the others present about what had happened. They were wonder-struck — they had just been asking Amma about God and miracles. Amma told me that I shouldn't have worried as She was planning to give darshan anyway. She then gave me an apple and asked me to eat it — Amma must have known that I hadn't eaten anything all day!

After darshan, we went down and the reporters came to interview me. Maybe that was why Amma had made me change into a clean shirt! She probably didn't want me to face the reporters when I was dirty. Amma does everything. She only wants us to surrender everything to God.

December 26th: I started working in the kitchen again. When I heard that Amma was giving darshan to those leaving that day, I went to the hall and sat right in front of Her. When it was my turn, I told Amma about my wife's pregnancy and the complications. She put Her hand on my head, blessed me and told me not to worry. That evening, my wife called me. She said that everything was fine, and told me to relax and enjoy my stay in Amma's ashram. The doctor had told her that he would perform the operation on January 4th, 2006.[1]

After darshan ended, Amma asked everyone to pray for the souls who had died in the tsunami that struck a year before. We were to walk in a procession to a place about two kilometers from the ashram. At that time, I had been helping another devotee clean the floor just below Amma's room. We decided to take Amma's chair and other necessary items to the site of the prayers. I noticed hand fans used for fanning Amma. I thought, how lucky it would be if Amma asks me to fan Her. I asked one of the devotees there if I could take the fans along as well. She readily agreed.

When we reached the site, one of the devotees there said that there was no point in bringing the fan as it was so breezy. She said that people would laugh if they saw those fans in my hand. I felt a little disappointed. I told her, "Let Amma decide whether She wants me to fan Her or not."

---

1 By Amma's grace, my wife gave birth to a healthy baby boy on the 4th.

After some time, Amma arrived. She planted some saplings and then sat on the chair we had brought. Then, to my surprise, She turned towards me and asked me to fan Her. I couldn't believe my ears! Anyone who could divine the heartfelt desires of a person had to be divine! I was in such a state of shock that when Amma again turned to me and tried to pass me the mike so that I could sing along, I just couldn't respond. She tried passing me the mike twice, but I couldn't respond. I was too overwhelmed by Amma's grace.

(April 2006)

Divine Protection
N. Vasudevan, Nigeria

Faith is beyond logic. When one has faith, one sees coincidences as miracles. If one does not, even the biggest miracle strikes one as a mere coincidence. Faith opens our eyes to miracles.

Ever since Amma came into my life and the lives of my family members about 25 years ago, a series of events has taken place in my life. Initially, I did not see anything out of the ordinary in these events. I would like to share just three instances that cannot, by any stretch of imagination, be considered coincidences.

I have been living in Africa for almost four decades. Our first darshan of Amma was in Boston, USA, about 24 years ago. My family was visiting the US for my son's school admission. I was not keen on darshan but agreed under intense pressure from my wife. Ever since, we have been devotees.

In 2003, while in India on an unscheduled visit, I went to Amritapuri for darshan, but Amma was not there. Waiting for Her to return would delay my departure to Nigeria by four days, and I was most reluctant to do this. After a lot of wavering, I decided to stay. I had a happy darshan. A day before my departure, I received a call from Nigeria informing me that armed robbers had broken into the apartment complex I lived in, killed one of our security guards, beaten up all the residents, and looted all their belongings. They had also broken open my flat, but the damage done was very small. I was lucky not to have faced them. I was happy and relieved but never seriously believed there was an invisible force protecting me.

In September 2007, I was on a holiday in India. As my return flight to Lagos could not be confirmed in time, my departure had to be delayed by a week because there were no flights for three days in a week and no available seat on the other days. My departure, which had been scheduled for September 8th, was delayed until the 13th. I was upset and angry. On the eve of my departure, i.e. on September 12th, I received a call from a colleague in Lagos who informed me that on the night before, owing to some electrical problems, fire from the air-conditioning unit in my bedroom had gutted the whole apartment. As this had started in the night, very little could be done to contain the fire and smoke. I was told that I had been very lucky not to have been in the apartment then because, even before facing the fire, I would have encountered heavy fumes and would not have escaped the bedroom alive. Everybody said I was very lucky, and I did not think beyond that.

All my items were reduced to ash except for three things, which were found almost intact on the floor:

1. A picture of Lord Ganapati, Remover of Obstacles. It had been kept in a wooden shelf that was reduced to ash, but

this picture remained untouched. Only its bottom edge looked a little charred.

2. A photo of Amma hanging on the wall; there was only a slight tinge of smoke on it.

3. An issue of *Mountain Path* featuring a picture of Ramana Maharshi, which had been kept on top of a bookshelf.

Some people said that the wind might have knocked these items to the floor. This does not explain why no other item had been spared. Also, how was it that everything else in the wooden shelf, including the shelf itself, had been burnt to a crisp except for the picture of Lord Ganapati?

The third incident happened in 2013, and it led me to believe that these events are not just coincidences.

We have factories in a city called Ibadan, which is about 2,000 feet above sea level. There are apartments perched on a hillock inside the factory complex. My apartment is on the top (second) floor. I spend a week in Ibadan every two months on official work. I was at Ibadan from February 16th, 2013, for four days and nights. At around 11 p.m. on the 16th, there was a strong gale and heavy downpour. At our height, the gale was particularly fierce. I could hardly see outside because the clouds were dark, but I heard the loud noise of falling trees. The noise levels kept increasing until it felt as if 20 trains were hurtling past our windows! I could not get any signal on my phones. I tried to open the sliding windows but failed because of the strong force of wind from the opposite direction. I soon started hearing the noises of falling roofs and boulders. I tried to open the bedroom door, but it was jammed. After intense effort and a prayer in panic, I managed to pry open the door only to find that the adjoining roof had been blown away and a flood of water was entering my room. The other bedroom as well as the living and dining rooms were facing an open sky and a very heavy downpour. There were live electric wires all over the place. I had no choice but to wade through the water in order to get to the ground floor to seek some help in switching off the electricity connection, and then to wait patiently for the morning.

The damage was extensive. Except for my bedroom, the rest of the roof and the concrete girders supporting the roof had fallen down. Architects and building engineers came and said the repairs would take a minimum of three weeks and that the roof over my bedroom would collapse any time. They advised me to vacate immediately. I had work to do and felt more comfortable staying in one place. As my stay there was for only three more nights and because the rains had stopped, I refused, saying the worst was over. I stayed in the same room for the next three days and nights. Food was brought up to me and I ate candle-lit dinners under an open sky.

My stubbornness upset, surprised and irritated my colleagues. I do not know what made me stay on—ignorance, foolhardiness or simply the fact that I felt comfortable working there. Every morning for the next three days, my colleagues would visit to check if the roof on my bedroom was still intact and if I was still alive.

On the fourth day, after finishing my work at Ibadan, I left for Lagos. The next morning, I received a call from the financial controller of the company in Ibadan. He said that the roof over my bedroom had collapsed the previous night along with the concrete girders supporting it.

Everybody around me wondered what had kept the roof intact for four days and why it fell only after I left, and that, too, without any rain or thunderstorm to provoke the collapse. I told them that I have a divine umbrella, which I may not truly deserve, protecting me from harm.

My colleagues, who are mainly Shiite Muslims from Lebanon, are now aware of Amma. They have seen Her photo and have heard me talking about Her. Though they have not professed devotion towards Amma, whenever any problem occurs, they immediately ask me, "Why don't you speak to your Amma about it? She will be able to help us!" Through such innocent remarks, I have begun to realize that Amma's outreach is much greater than I have ever imagined. Such is Her love, which emanates even from Her photo, that it touches the lives of all those who come into contact with Her. May Amma's protection bless us all!

(October 2016)

Mata Pita Press
Lalitha Unny, India

Ammuma,[1] as she is popularly known in the Amritapuri ashram, sits on the veranda of the Amritanjali block, a benign smile on her gentle face. She had previously been a Sai Baba devotee, and had already been given a mantra. So when Ammuma asked Amma for a mantra, Amma told her to continue chanting the one she had.

Before she came to the ashram, Ammuma had many spiritual experiences, such as hearing the sound of the inner flute. But Amma told her to focus more on Parashakti[2] and not to give too much importance to experiences.

Watching Amma during Devi Bhava darshans, Ammuma would often see Her changing into the terrifying Kali form. As soon as Amma noticed that Ammuma was uncomfortable, She would reveal Her smiling Krishna form and then resume Her Devi Bhava. Very often when she sat behind Amma on Devi Bhava days, she would see a blinding flash of light very close to Amma. If she fell asleep during archana, she found that Amma would wake her up in some way; either someone would pinch her or make enough noise to awaken her.

---

1 'Grandmother' in Malayalam.

2 Supreme Power, personified as the Goddess.

Ammuma's husband, Acchan[3] (as he was called), believed more in meditation than in archana. He also had strong faith in Amma. One day after coming to the ashram, he found that he could not move his hands properly. When he spoke to Amma about it, She told him that the problem was not with his hands but with his brain. After examining him, the doctors told him that he had a small tumor in his brain. As a result, eventually, his body became totally paralyzed. For three months, he lay bed-ridden. During that period, Amma would repeatedly inquire about his well-being. She also instructed Ammuma to read the *Bhagavatam*[4] to him continuously. A few minutes before his passing, Amma came personally into the room and poured a little of the sacred Ganges water into his mouth. Acchan's good friend, Mr. Nair, had passed away a few days before. Amma said that Mr. Nair had been waiting for Acchan to join him. When Acchan breathed his last, Amma said that he had attained moksha. She closed his eyes and set his body in the right position. Looking out through the window, She said, "Look at him laughing now! He's freed of his ego. He knows the truth now." Amma also said that She was talking to Acchan in Her

---

3 'Father' in Malayalam.

4 Also known as *Srimad Bhagavatam* or *Bhagavata Purana* (meaning 'Sacred Tales of the Supreme Lord'), one of the Puranic texts of Hinduism. Contains stories of Vishnu, including the life and pastimes of Krishna.

heart. She wanted his body to be covered in the ochre robes of a *sanyasi* (ordained monk) before he was taken for the last rites. With so many blessings from Amma, Ammuma did not experience any grief after his death.

When Amma came into her room again later, Ammuma had nothing to offer Her. So, she quickly went to a neighboring room and obtained some milk and snacks, which Amma distributed as prasad to all those who were there. Amma's visit and Her soothing words made even death a celebration.

Ammuma recollects another incident. A Tamil-speaking Brahmin woman would come to her house every *Dwadashi* day[5] and accept some uncooked food from her. However, she would neither eat any food in the house nor enter it. She would sit outside in the veranda. This woman was illiterate and could not speak in any other language.

Years before she met Amma, Ammuma had developed a strong aversion to housework. She wished only to read spiritual books or listen to bhajans and dance to them. She was so unhappy with her lot that she wrote a letter and kept it behind the picture of Devi on her altar. In this letter, she asked Devi, "What should a woman do if she is married but does not want to do any housework? Her heart is full of *bhakti* (devotion) and she just wants to pray." Sitting on the raised platform in the

5 The 12th day of the bright or dark fortnight of every lunar month.

veranda, Ammuma wept and prayed, "O Amma Parashakti! Answer my question!"

She was stunned when the Tamil Brahmin woman suddenly emerged from inside her house and started a discourse on *stree dharma*, the duty of a woman. However, it did not occur to Ammuma to question the woman then. The talk began without any preamble. She was told that a pure woman brings sanctity to the house. Besides, a married woman cannot hold God with both hands; one hand is for God, whereas the other is for karma. A woman's duty was always to treat a husband well — to receive him with a smile when he returned from work and to offer him a drink. She should never complain about her husband to anyone. As the Brahmin woman was speaking, a beggar came to the door. Ammuma got up to give her some food. The Brahmin woman was very pleased and said, "This is also the duty of a householder: to treat a beggar as God."

The Brahmin woman then started speaking about the *Guru-sishya* (Master-disciple) relationship. She narrated a story about a disciple who used to beg for alms and feed his Guru regularly, as a result of which he acquired many occult powers. The sishya became egoistic and started ignoring his Guru. When he went out the next time, he saw that all his firewood had turned into metal. Anxious at this turn of events, he went back to his Guru, who told him that his ego had caused this aberration.

After this discourse, the Brahmin woman left only to return the next day, asking for food. Ammuma was a little surprised, because she had never eaten in her house before. Nevertheless, Ammuma was very happy and fed the woman well. This time, the woman asked her if she had a copy of the *Devi Mahatmyam*.[6] When Ammuma said no, the woman went away, saying that she would get her a copy the next day. True to her word, she brought the book and told Ammuma to read four verses from it daily without fail. Ammuma followed her instructions, keeping the book with her until she lost it in a hospital, where she had to undergo an operation. She tried very hard to find another copy but failed since both the printing press (Mata Pita Press) and the editor (Govindan Namboodiri) were non-existent.

After a few days, the Brahmin woman came to Ammuma's house and was very annoyed when asked about her earlier visits. She denied having come there at all, and when Ammuma offered her tea, she refused to have any. It was only then that Ammuma was able to put all the pieces of the puzzle together. She realized that her visitor had been none other than Parashakti Herself!

---

6 700 verses glorifying the Divine Mother.

Years later, when she met Amma, she realized that Amma was the Parashakti whom she had worshipped all along. Amma's frequent references to stree dharma in Her discourses fortified her belief.

Now, Ammuma sits comfortably in front of her room, listening to discourses and bhajans, tranquil at the thought of being cradled by Amma, and relaxed in the company of her children and grandchildren; they are all here, permanently settled in the ashram, three generations devoted to Amma, contentment writ large on their faces.

(November 2013)

Anointed
Sharadamani, India

I was born into a family of Sri Ramakrishna Paramahamsa devotees, and it was only natural that I was exposed to His teachings while young. As a child, I used to read His books repeatedly and feel sad that I had not been His contemporary. When I met a person who spoke to me about Amma — Her divine moods, the miracles She performed, and how She had licked the wounds of the leper Dattan to cure him — I was not really impressed. However, I sensed that Amma was an extraordinary phenomenon and prayed fervently to Ramakrishna Paramahamsa to throw some light on this marvel: was she or was she not a divine incarnation?

Soon thereafter, I came across a book on Amma, 'Yagna Prasadam,' written by Ottoor Unni Namboodiri, the author of Amma's *Ashtottaram* (108 attributes). In it, he wrote that Amma was enacting in Amritapuri the same divine drama that Sri Ramakrishna Paramahamsa and Sri Sharada Devi, His consort, had enacted in Dakshineswar more than 100 years ago. Reading this, I felt that I had to meet Amma at once.

My husband and I went to see Her and joined the darshan line. Imagine my surprise when someone came to reshuffle the queue, and we emerged standing right in front of Amma! During that first meeting with Amma, I broke down and cried, unable to stop the torrent of my tears. Who can explain the presence of God, the bliss that pulses in the heart when it finally reaches its goal? I told myself, "I am Amma's child now!"

When Sri Ramakrishna Paramahamsa was about to leave His mortal body, on seeing the pain of His devotees, He had promised that he would return to a place surrounded by water, that a lot of 'white' devotees would come to Him, and that He would resume His divine mission then. My conviction that Amma was indeed Ramakrishna Paramahamsa and Sharada Devi combined propelled me towards Her like nothing else.

My elder son joined the ashram as a brahmachari when there was an acute shortage of food, water and proper accommodation. As a result, my son, who had known no hunger, became emaciated. My mind wept in pain, and I turned to one of Amma's books — a habit I had of opening the book at random and finding the answer to my problems. The following lines stared at me: "My children should be thin, with their stomachs caved in. Only then will their faces shine, making them look like courageous lions. Their inner spiritual bliss must be reflected on their faces." My heart missed a beat. How blessed I was to have a son like him! In this way, Amma severed the bond of attachment I had for my son. I could see clearly that he was Amma's son.

In 2001, my younger son, Sudeep, met with an accident and was admitted to AIMS Hospital in a serious condition. I would finish my ashram seva by afternoon and visit him every evening. On the third day, the brahmacharis attending to him found that the top of his head had become very soft. When I ran my fingers over his head, I found that they were right. We immediately contacted the doctors, who said that he might need to undergo emergency surgery of the skull.

On returning to the ashram, I cried myself to sleep, pleading with Amma to intervene. I had a very vivid dream. I was standing in front of a Devi temple and the doors to the *sanctum sanctorum* were closed as I waited. Suddenly, the doors opened and a *pujari* (priest) came out and poured liquid ghee on the crown of my head. The experience was so real that I could feel the ghee for a long time after I woke up. I felt that this was a message from Amma, though I was unable to decipher its meaning. I did not tell anyone about the dream.

As usual, I went for my seva the next morning and reached the hospital by evening. My son and his attendant looked happy. The attendant said, "Something wonderful happened yesterday. Touch his head now. It's hard again, not soft like it was yesterday. Amma rang up last night and asked, 'How is Sudeep?' When I told Her what the doctors had said, Amma said, 'No operation! Give the phone to Sudeep.' She asked him, 'How are you? No need to worry. Amma is with you. Kisses to you!'"

The next morning, a team of doctors arrived at 9:00 a.m., each one looking for the tender spot on his head. There was no trace of it! Sudeep's head was as hard as a head should be! When the doctors left, I told everyone about my dream.

I would like to mention a few among the innumerable occasions when Amma fulfilled my heartfelt desires.

In my garden, there used to be an old jackfruit tree that bore excellent fruit. One year, I plucked three of the biggest jackfruits, intending to offer them to Amma that weekend. However, my son came down with high fever, forcing me to cancel my trip to the ashram. I was bitterly disappointed. I cried a lot and told myself, "Amma has so many children. Why should She care about me and my little gift?"

While crying, a car screeched to a halt in front of our house. An acquaintance stepped out and said, "I was passing by on my way to the ashram, when I felt an irresistible urge to ask you if you would like to accompany me." Amma had heard my prayer! I realized that Amma cannot bear to see Her children in tears. If I could not take the fruits to Her, She would come and take them from me! Off I went to get the fruits and load them into his car.

In the early years of the ashram, the morning archana used to take place in the *kalari*, the temple where Amma used to give Devi Bhava and Krishna Bhava darshans. Bri. (Dr.) Leela (now Swamini Atma Prana) used to lead the archana, and the rest would respond. One day, she started coughing badly and turned around to ask the woman behind her if she could take over. This woman refused and Bri. Leela continued with great difficulty. I wanted to take over, but did not dare to ask. I kept my desire a secret. Imagine my surprise when Bri. Leela came running the next day to the meditation hut, where we were all sitting together, and said, "Amma has asked you to lead the archana today." I thought, "Me? A mere householder to lead the archana?" Later, I learned that Amma had come down from Her room and stood for some time, listening to me as I led the archana.

Countless are the occasions when Amma has shown that She cares, that She is aware of every thought that passes through Her child's mind, and that She is always willing to fulfill all those little desires that will keep us away from trouble and lead us closer to Her.

(March 2016)

Saving Grace

Healed by Amma

Yusuf Husayn Abdullah, U.K.

I was an only child raised in the slums of Manchester, England, by my father, a Turkish Muslim, and my mother, a half-English, half-Irish, devout Roman Catholic. My father was a strict disciplinarian, who wanted no evidence of Christianity in his home. He was also an alcoholic. The result was plenty of conflict and a frequently violent family life that made living at home difficult. For much of my childhood, I survived by living in the streets.

On one particular occasion, in a drunken rage, my father beat my mother terribly. Though I was only four then, I felt I could not stand by and watch this without trying to stop it. But when I tried, he began to beat me, finally throwing me against a wall with such force that I received severe injuries. From then on, I suffered from frequent epileptic seizures, which included severe asthmatic attacks during which I could not exhale, only inhale, with the result that my face would turn completely blue. I would inevitably be hospitalized. Medication only served to reduce the duration of the seizures; it did not avert them altogether.

It was not until I was 31 that Mother's grace first shone on my life (at least as far as I know). I had previously been recruited into the Iranian army. The day after receiving my first post, to which I had to report in two weeks, I left for a quick trip to Europe. A friend suggested I go to the Center Of Unity in Brienz, Switzerland, for information relating to a doctoral thesis in philosophy. Little did I know that Mother would arrive at this very Center while I was there. Naturally, my curiosity over the visiting woman saint led me to see Her.

I had no particular feeling for Mother as my Guru at this time, but my first darshan changed the direction of my life. As I stood up from Mother's loving embrace, I felt almost drunk — weak-kneed and dizzy. I couldn't even see clearly. In fact, I noticed I could see more clearly with my eyes closed! I saw what I can only describe as the light bodies of everyone present, with points of lights within their bodies. I also saw everyone's aura clearly, all with eyes closed. I didn't know what was happening to me.

When I returned to England, I decided not to serve in the Iranian army. I took the suitcase the army had given me and which contained my uniform, passbook, military log book, etc., and left it in the main Shiite mosque in London. I was still unable to understand my experience with Amma, however. In an effort to understand it, I described my experience to a Muslim friend whom I respected. He told me that I'd been affected by a jinn, by black magic. This didn't ring true to me, but created enough doubt about Mother that I decided to forget about Her. Forgetting about Mother, I soon discovered, is not so easy.

One night a few months later, I had an extraordinarily vivid dream. In my dream, I traveled by train to a mosque, where I prayed. I then sat down to read the Koran. As I finished the first chapter, I looked up with tired eyes and saw, above me, a beautiful, brilliant being — a divine woman radiating the purest light of holiness. She wore a red sari and bright, shining crown. Her face was Mother's.

I couldn't believe what I was seeing. It was so vivid it could not be simply a dream. Mother had six arms, and was smiling. Her lower left hand, with the OM sign, came around and summoned me towards Her. Then I felt myself tugged forward very sharply, as if by a rope. I fell on my head, and at that point I had the feeling of being snapped back into my body — as if my dream had literally taken me out of my body. I woke up.

This 'dream' made me suspect I was going crazy. I made an appointment with a psychiatrist. This psychiatrist, however, told me that he'd studied the paranormal for years, and in his opinion I should not be overly concerned about my dream. Rather, he suggested that I try to obey what it was telling me to do.

This I did. I went back to Brienz in 1989 to see Mother again. As Mother got out of the car, She looked at me, and smiling with motherly love, said a few words to the interpreter, who translated for me: "Mother says that She is very glad you could make it." At these words, seeing Her beneficent, charming smile, it was clear to me that the woman before me, and the Divine

Being in my 'dream' were one and the same. The reality of this was more awe-inspiring than I can express. I burst into tears.

During my stay in Brienz that year, Mother invited me to come to India, to Her ashram. Within a few months, I found myself on a plane to India. I had many experiences with Mother in Her own home. But four weeks after my arrival, in the darshan hut, Mother gave me the darshan that would change my life forever. She ran Her hand up and down my back for what seemed like several minutes. At one point, I felt a powerful tremor throughout my body. Since that day, my seizures of 31 years never recurred; nor have I ever had another attack of asthma. And never have I since doubted this: Mother is Devi. All Glory to Her!

(February 1995)

Saving Grace
Swapna Dayanandan, Singapore

We are a family of four — my parents, my younger brother and myself. Being devout, our parents tried to instill devotion to God, and love and respect for our elders, in my brother and me right from the time we were young. Besides sending us to religious classes for children, our parents also ensured that we did daily prayers at home, both in the mornings and evenings. However, we never had any prior experience with a spiritual master, and had only read in books about the stories and experiences of Gurus.

Our first experience with Amma in the year 1989 was astounding. My younger brother was then 15 years old. Even as a child, he disliked being hugged and would feel irritated if anyone hugged him. When he heard that Amma hugged those who went for darshan, he hesitated to go. After persistent persuasion by my mother, he reluctantly accompanied us for Amma's darshan.

During darshan, Amma gazed at him lovingly and said, "Darling, your mother had to persuade you to come to Amma, didn't she?" We were all astounded by Amma's question. Amma continued, "My darling child! It is your age that makes you dislike this. But there will come a time when you will yearn for such an opportunity (to receive Amma's blessings)." Neither my brother nor I understood the significance of Amma's words then.

On our very first darshan in 1989, Amma won us over completely. Amma's loving gaze and consoling hug melted our hearts and kindled faith in God. At that time, we were unaware that Amma is a manifestation of the Supreme. We thought Amma was a saint or spiritual teacher. Since then, we have never missed Amma's darshan in Singapore every year. We also started attending the monthly bhajans and, later on, the weekly discourses and bhajans as well. We began to feel that we were being drawn closer to Amma. We anxiously looked forward to Amma's arrival year after year with more and more yearning. We also became more involved in organizing Amma's birthday celebrations and Her programs in Singapore.

Amma's visit to our home in November 1993 was a remarkable and unforgettable occasion in our life. Earlier in March that year, we also had the blessing of Amma's first sanyasi disciple, Swami Amritaswarupanandaji, visiting our home.

We started the New Year 1995 with our usual New Year's Eve party with a small group of family friends. Little did we know what was in stock for us. If not for Amma's grace, 1995 would have ushered darkness into our lives.

In the first week of January 1995, my mother was diagnosed with drop attack epilepsy. The neurologist prescribed tablets, and my mother took these for about 12 days. On the 10th day of her medication, my mother came down with a bad flu. As our family doctor's clinic was closed that day, we consulted another doctor, who is also a good family friend. As my mother had no known history of drug allergy, she was prescribed antibiotics that she had never taken before.

On the morning of the 12th day on her medication, my mother vomited blood. My father was leaving for work, and I was about to leave for college. My mother vomited blood again and became unconscious.

While doctors were attending to my mother, I thought, "Amma, how gracious You are! If this had happened after my father and I left the house, my mother would have been in a helpless situation."

For the first five days, the doctors said that my mother's condition was unstable. They were not sure of the internal injury. Later, a doctor explained that my mother had developed a severe drug allergy known as Steven-Johnson Syndrome, which has a mortality rate of 70%. The medicine for her mild epilepsy, which caused the allergic reaction, had high sulfur content. It was plain bad luck that the antibiotics aggravated the condition. On recovery, 50% of the patients suffer from permanent blindness, and 40%, from kidney failure. The prognosis was so bleak that I easily gave in to despair. The pathetic state of my mother further fuelled my despair, and my hope of ever seeing her alive and well, diminished day by day. She looked like a patient with third-degree burns. She had ulcers on her lips and her entire stomach. She was put on drips for nearly two weeks. Her diet for the next two months consisted of food that had to be finely ground and blended. The doctors were afraid that the large blisters that covered her body might burst and expose the flesh beneath. This would cause my mother indescribable pain, and she would have to be covered with plastic sheets. I shuddered at the very thought. My family felt helpless, and we prayed whole-heartedly to Amma to shower Her grace on my mother.

Everyone in Amma's satsang prayed for us. They helped us through this period of great suffering by rendering assistance in many ways — being with us in the hospital, offering comforting words, and, most importantly, praying sincerely for my mother's recovery.

The intense prayers from everyone paved the way for a miracle, which came about by Amma's grace. During an evening darshan at the Thiruvananthapuram ashram, Amma asked one of the ashram residents to call Rajan Menon in Singapore (while in Singapore, Amma stays with Mr. and Mrs. Menon and their family). Amma wanted to know if everything was alright in Singapore. Rajan Menon informed the ashram resident that my mother was in serious condition, and to convey this message to Amma.

From that day, things took a turn for the better. My mother was slowly but surely on the road to recovery. She was then, and is even now, a medical wonder to all the doctors who attended to her. She recovered completely without any side effect of the Steven Johnson Syndrome. The miraculous thing was that my mother was spared of much pain. Her blisters healed well without bursting and the dried skin shed off painlessly. At that time, she looked very much like a peeled onion!

A month after she was discharged, my mother went to Amritapuri for Amma's darshan. At that time, my mother was gripped with a fear of taking medication. She was emotionally and psychologically scarred from her terrible ordeal. Amma's affectionate darshans allayed her fear and instilled courage in her.

On December 29th, 1995, my mother made a second trip to Amritapuri. Because of the New Year, there was a large crowd in the ashram and thus insufficient accommodation. My mother was asked to share a room with other devotees. Owing to her poor health, my mother developed a sore throat, and by the next morning, her face had become swollen. Amma noticed my mother from a distance and called her. Amma looked surprised to see my mother so ill, and asked if she had been given proper accommodation. My mother explained the situation to Amma, who immediately summoned a brahmacharini and asked her to give my mother either a single room or special accommodation in a hut, saying, "Do you know that this child has just recovered from a serious illness, and that she resembles a peeled onion?"

When my mother called from Amritapuri to tell me what Amma had said, I asked, "How could Amma, who was never told about the details of your illness, know what your condition is like?"

My mother replied, *"Ellam ariyunna ammayode onnum parayenda karyamilla."* Her words were actually lines from a bhajan — "There is no need to say anything to Amma, who knows everything." Our experience taught us that if we have complete faith in Amma, Her grace will always be available, during both good and bad times.

(February 1997)

Gift of Fate
Prem, India

Sitting in the shade of a tree, Dr. Anantanarayanan related his story. His memory was brimming with the blissful experiences Amma had bestowed on him during a period of great suffering.

Anantanarayanan first met Amma in 1984, but he had a feeling that theirs was a relationship that stretched back through many lifetimes. Still, he felt his bond with Amma deepening with each passing day.

In 1987, destiny started to batter Anantanarayanan with its cruel fists. He had a heart attack, which left him feeling depressed. Luckily, Amma's soothing love helped him tide over this period. As soon as he had emerged from this dark period, fate dealt him another harsh blow. It was Anantanarayanan's habit to go for a walk every morning while chanting his mantra, in order to refresh himself both physically and mentally. On the morning of May 11, 1990, while taking his walk, a newspaper van knocked into him, throwing him several feet in the air. He was rushed to the hospital, where a scan revealed blood clots in the upper left part of his brain.

As he lay in a coma, his family and friends grieved. They didn't think he would survive. The doctors then discovered that his left arm was fractured. They operated on the arm, and a steel rod was inserted into it.

Amma, who was on Her World Tour then, was informed about his condition. She sent him a consoling message: "My darling son, don't worry. Everything will be all right. Don't lose heart." When the message arrived, Anantanarayanan emerged from the coma, but continued drifting in and out of consciousness. Amma's message was read to him when he seemed awake. Amma's message of hope surprised the doctors because they didn't think he would ever get his memory back, let alone walk.

Miraculously, 16 days after the surgery, his memory slowly began to return. A few days later, Swami Amritageetananda visited him. The visit greatly uplifted Anantanarayanan, who had been feeling dispirited and helpless. He felt a new glow of hope being kindled within him. As he lay there, he felt Amma's merciful arms reaching out towards him. From then on, Amma's name and memories of Her started to dance in his mind; he was conscious only of Amma. Day and night, he lost himself in the sacred mantra, "Amma." He seemed to float on the waves of Mother's overflowing love and compassion. He felt Mother sitting beside him on the bed, caressing him and whispering in his ears, "Don't worry, son. Amma is with you."

A month later, he began to recognize people's faces and remember their names, much to everyone's surprise.

But his joy did not last for long. The arm that had been operated on became infected. The doctors decided to remove the steel rod; but as it was being removed, almost an inch of the bone in that arm was shattered. He was taken to the Thrissur Medical College for further treatment.

After all that suffering, fate still refused to leave the doctor and his family alone. His daughter reacted adversely to the sulfur in medication she had taken for fever. Her body became covered with blisters, and her eyes became badly infected. It was the dreaded Stephen-Johnson syndrome. Her body became a terrible sight. Anantanarayanan bore this additional blow of fate calmly. Even during this trial, he could still hear Amma's comforting words deep within: "Amma is with you, son. Don't worry." These words gave him the strength to withstand all the cruelties of fate.

Anantanarayanan's colleagues felt that his daughter should be taken to the All India Institute of Medical Sciences in New Delhi for further tests. Before leaving for New Delhi, his daughter visited Amma, who hugged her and whispered, "Darling daughter, don't worry!" Amma then suggested that she cancel the trip to Delhi. She followed Amma's advice, and gradually recovered from her illness.

The doctor's injured arm was still dysfunctional. The doctors felt that bone grafting was necessary. Anantanarayanan sought Amma's advice. She asked about the treatment. After that, Amma gently stroked the injured arm and said, "Son, you don't need any more surgery. Everything will be all right." At first, Anantanarayanan found it difficult to believe what

Amma was saying; for, as a medical doctor, he knew that the chances of the shattered bone segment healing by itself were slim, and that it would take a long time for the bone segment to regain its shape. Nevertheless, he had the unshakeable faith that Mother's *sankalpa* (divine resolve) would bear fruit. He decided not to go ahead with the operation. His arm soon began functioning normally, much to the bafflement of the doctors.

Anantanarayanan started working as a doctor again. As service to Mother, he also offers free medical services. He is the brain behind the free medical camp, which is conducted regularly in many ashram branches.

We had been sitting under the tree for quite some time. The tree's cooling shadow had moved away, but my mind found relief from the scorching heat of worldliness in the refreshing coolness of the doctor's narration. Anantanarayanan stood up and softly said, "By Amma's grace, I have been reborn." There was a glow on his face, the peaceful glow of someone who accepts his fate as a precious gift from God.

(June 1997)

Watching Over Us
Santosh (Sunny Nell), USA

On Thursday, June 18th, 2009, a week before the scheduled Caesarean section, my wife and I went to the hospital for her weekly stress test and to confirm the baby's well-being. That morning, my wife noticed that the baby was not moving much. At 10 a.m., the nurses began the stress test, which continued for 45 minutes. The doctor then told us, "As the baby is not responding as it should, we think you should go to the hospital for an ultrasound."

At 1:25 p.m. the radiology technician began the ultrasound test. All this time, my wife was feeling a bit uneasy, even though she was trying to be cheerful. After almost 45 minutes into the test, the technician typed on the screen: 'Baby not breathing for the last 45 minutes.' When I saw this, I asked the technician for more details. She said that it happens sometimes, and then ushered us to the waiting room, saying that the doctor would talk to us soon. After 10 minutes, the doctor called to say that my wife should head to the birthing center immediately. She also said that she would make arrangements to get us there.

We waited for almost 20 more minutes but nothing happened. So we decided to walk slowly towards the elevator that would take us to the birthing center, which was on the 4th floor. When we reached the birthing center, we realized that the doctors, nurses and a team of specialists were waiting to take my wife into the surgery room for an immediate C-section. The team started administering IV fluids and inducing anesthesia. At this point, the lead surgeon (my wife's doctor) came into the triage area and told me that as the baby was not doing well, the surgery needed to be performed immediately. She explained that a baby's USG (ultrasonography) rating should be 8 or above, and that if it falls below 6, then the procedure is to immediately perform surgery to deliver the baby. In my baby's case, the reading was below 2! She continued to say that we may have lost the baby already and needed to try to save the mom, as she was also sinking.

The doctor then asked me the dreaded question: "If we have a choice, whom should we save?"

My obvious response was "The mother." At this point, I bowed my head in prayer to Amma. She was then in LA as part of her Summer Tour. Since we live in Minnesota, we had not had the opportunity to meet Her yet during this tour. I prayed to Her, "When I return home from hospital today, I may have lost my partner, and my kids may have lost their mother and their little brother. I cannot change what is destined. Only You can. Please be present during the surgery, and take care of the situation. Give me the strength to accept whatever happens as Your will." With a new-found strength I had acquired through prayer, and a deep conviction that nothing would go wrong, I called a couple of friends to update them on the situation. I could sense them getting nervous when they heard what was going on but they assured me that everything would be fine. They said they would come to the hospital as soon as possible.

The doctor then mentioned that a second surgeon had been called in to assist, and that they would begin the surgery as soon as he arrived. Three minutes later, the assisting surgeon arrived, and the team began the surgery at approximately 3:55 p.m. At 4:31 p.m. the baby was delivered. The pediatrician checked and reported the baby was safe and that all vital signs were responding well! The team then continued to work on my wife, and finally completed the process at about 5:45 p.m. The lead surgeon then came out and said to me, "You are very lucky. You have someone watching over you. In my 20 years of practice, I have never seen a baby with a USG rating of 2 survive!"

Later, the baby was moved to the nursery and my wife was moved to the suite for post-surgical care. On Sunday, the lead surgeon came to complete the discharge process and said to my wife, "I'm not sure who performed this miracle. You have someone watching over you, and that same person watched over me while I performed the surgery. Had it not been for this divine power, it would have been a different story!"

Throughout that Thursday afternoon, I kept Amma informed through Br. Dayamrita Chaitanya. I also called him as soon as the baby was born to let Amma know. I asked Br. Dayamritaji to ask Amma for a name for my child. When he asked Amma, She told him that she wanted us to come to Chicago with the baby, and that She would name him there. On the twelfth day after the surgery, we boarded the Amtrak and travelled eight hours to Chicago. Some people we knew were shocked that we were traveling so soon after the surgery, afraid that it would be unsafe for both mother and child. My thought was, "If Amma can give my child life, she can surely take care of him and my wife during a train ride!"

When Amma received the baby during darshan, she asked me to verify his birth star with the astrologer (traveling with Amma). I had initially told her that his birth star was 'Revati,' and as I understood later, the time of birth would have been very inauspicious, a threat to his very life. Amma's immediate reaction had been that a *Mrityunjaya Homa* (a rite performed to prolong life) be performed immediately and then every year thereafter. After consulting the astrologer, we realized that the child had been born after the inauspicious time had passed, and that the birth star was actually 'Ashwati.' When we told Amma this, She sighed with relief and said, "When you first told me about the birth star and time, Amma was worried, but now everything is fine, as the time of birth is good, and Ashwati is a very good birth star." Amma gazed at the baby adoringly and kissed him before handing him back to me. Amma then asked us to sit next to Her, and She continued looking at the baby several times. Finally, She named him "Amrit or Amarath," which means 'Immortal.'

During this period, our devotee friends helped us in many ways, for which we are thankful. During our post-partum visit to the doctor after four weeks, the first thing the doctor said on seeing us was, "Here comes the blessed family, who has someone watching over them. I feel lucky to have known you guys!" Saying so, she gave us a hug.

Indeed, Amma has been watching over us, and it was Her blessings alone that saved my wife and son! Amma, please accept our humble thanks.

(December 2009)

My Secret

M. Ramakrishnan, U.S.A.

I met Amma in 1987 in India. My whole family is devoted to Amma. She transformed me from one who merely believed in Her into one who has strong faith in Her. The difference between faith and belief is this: faith is firm, whereas belief can waver. In order to bring about this change in me, Amma resorted to a miracle.

One day in 1991, during Devi Bhava darshan, Amma asked me a strange question: would I mind going abroad to study and work? I didn't know what to say. Firstly, I did not have enough money. Secondly, I had a good job close to home, and could visit Amma twice or thrice a week. Yet, my circumstances changed soon after, and I found myself going to the USA for studies at the Arizona State University. Though surprised, I remembered the saying that whatever a mahatma says comes true in due course.

I had a tough time going back to school, that, too, in a new educational system and a new environment, but I had the faith that Amma was with me. I felt that I was not alone, and that whatever happened, Amma was supporting me at all times.

One morning, after my prayers to Amma, I left my apartment and went for my classes. Soon, my stomach started aching. At first, I thought it was because I had not eaten breakfast.

I went to a Taco Bell, the haunt of poor students like me, but that made things worse. By the time I reached my workplace, the stomach pain had become severe. I went to the health center, where I vomited. I felt a little better, but the nurses and doctors were moving around with troubled expressions on their faces, not telling me anything except, "You're going to be okay!" Finally, I asked them what the problem was. They said, "We don't really know. You neither have any blood pressure nor a heartbeat. You should be dead, but you are talking!" I was transferred to the nearest hospital and given some tests, which revealed I had acute pancreatitis, a disease typically found in older people who smoke and use drugs. They questioned me, and I told them that I had never smoked or taken drugs in my life. Not believing me, they asked my friends, who confirmed my statement. Later, when the pain worsened, I was transferred to the intensive care unit. Further tests revealed a basketball-sized cyst in my abdomen. It had become so big that I could hardly breathe. The doctors decided that I should not be given any food or water until the cyst shrank. Mine was a life-threatening situation. In fact, the doctors later told that they had almost lost me twice or thrice, but I somehow kept coming back. This was a mystery to them, but I knew the 'doctor' responsible for saving me!

The hospital contacted Bipin, my cousin's husband, in Seattle, and informed him that I was on the verge of death. He was asked for consent to use any procedure the hospital deemed necessary to save my life. He immediately called Amma's Mumbai ashram and spoke to Swami Pranavamritananda, who was just leaving for Delhi to see Amma there. He conveyed the message about my condition to Amma, who became silent and had a very distant look on Her face. She then said, "He will be okay. He doesn't need an operation for this." This message was conveyed to Bipin.

At the same time, my precarious condition began to improve, and by the time Bipin called the hospital, I was out of danger. Amma, doctor of the universe, had saved me.

After five weeks in the hospital without food or drink, the main surgeon decided to operate in order to drain the cyst. The other doctors didn't agree, saying that a number of people had recently died from the risky operation. The surgeon insisted and the date was fixed. The night before the surgery, two friends informed me that this surgeon had a bad reputation for insisting on surgery, even when it wasn't advisable. They called the surgeon and cancelled the operation. They were told of another doctor who could do an endoscopic procedure that could drain the cyst. This was arranged, and I was soon on the road to recovery.

Having had no prior experience of hospitals or emergencies, I should have been extremely agitated under the circumstances. Yet, I was calm, certain that I would not die. Hadn't Amma asked me to come to this country? She arranged many caring people to come and keep me company in the hospital so that I would not entertain unpleasant thoughts. I even made history by being the first person to be treated by the new endoscopic procedure, and the only patient to stay in the hospital for seven weeks without eating or drinking! The nurses felt I had some special mental strength to deal with all that I underwent here. I did; it is Amma!

(November 1997)

Primordial Doctor
Dr. V. Satyaprasad, India

Years ago, I used to see posters of Amma in Chennai, and I used to be attracted by Her cherubic smile. I felt that even in photos, She appeared to love people incessantly and unconditionally. I realized later that love was Her very nature, but the multi-faceted nature of Her love is unfathomable.

One night, during the first week of December 1996, my wife and I were feeling mentally agitated over a personal problem, and could not sleep. Suddenly, I recalled that Amma was visiting Chennai that week. We decided to have Her darshan, and drove to the Brahmasthanam Temple at Arcot Road. There was a very big queue of people encroaching upon the road and patiently waiting for their turn. It was raining then. I approached one of Amma's disciples, who arranged for our darshan.

Amma's darshan was the most delectable experience my wife and I ever had. Peace pervaded my whole being. During darshan, we forgot to tell Amma about our problem. Imagine my surprise when She started talking about the problem that was causing our agitation and said that She would solve the problem. We then went home peacefully.

A few weeks later, I received a call from a colleague asking me to assist in starting a new Cardiac Surgery Unit at the AIMS Hospital in Cochin, Kerala. I had thought that we had settled down in Chennai. My children were studying there, my wife and I were working in a well-equipped Cardiac Specialty Hospital, and we were living in our own house. Something deep within urged me to accept this opportunity to move to AIMS Hospital, which is a mahatma's offering to humanity. When I mentioned this to my parents, they, too, spontaneously agreed. Soon thereafter, my family moved to Cochin.

In hindsight, it is clear that Amma has been a guiding light in my personal and professional life. Once, I had almost decided that I would not operate on a patient, as the entire structure of his heart had become heavily calcified. However, when he told me that Amma had asked him to undergo surgery in AIMS Hospital, I felt emboldened to perform the surgery. When I opened the heart, even the chief anesthetist, who was standing next to me in the theater, looked at me in awe when he saw the precarious condition of the heart. But I had a feeling that it was Amma's decision to go ahead with the surgery and that She would see to its safe passage.

Everything happened as though it were pre-ordained. Though difficult, I performed the surgery quite smoothly, as if I were in a trance. The patient was extubated in less than 12 hours and was discharged from the hospital as a normal case on the eighth day. There were several such instances when I felt that I was only an instrument in Her hands. This fortified my belief in the saying, "The doctor only treats. It is God who heals." Since then, I always start surgery thinking about Her. Also, I do not get unduly perturbed about how things are going to unfold. I feel that all the ventures in the Cardiac Surgery Unit are in Her hands.

Above all, I feel immensely blessed in being able to perform several major heart surgeries for patients upon Amma's instructions. These patients would not otherwise have been able to afford the surgery. Her compassion for the poor is so evident from the fact that She keeps encouraging me to perform as many such surgeries as possible.

Amma has also been a tremendous source of encouragement to patients who were apprehensive about undergoing major cardiac surgeries. After getting Her darshan and blessings, I have seen them courageously facing what is usually a traumatic experience. This is, no doubt, the result of Her divine grace. It is rewarding to see them looking so happy and grateful when discharged from the hospital.

Amma has also been a mentor creating cohesion, teamwork and harmony in the Cardiac Surgery Unit. I pray that She continues to bless us in all our endeavors.

(October 2003)

Rebirth
E. Shanta Krishnankutty, India

saandraanandaavabodhaatmakamanupamitam kaala-
deshaavadhibhyaam
nirmuktam nityamuktam nigamashatasahasrena nir-
bhaasyamaanam
aspashtam drshtamaatre punarurupurushaarthaatmakam
brahmatatvam...
She is of the nature of unbroken bliss and supreme consciousness, incomparable, and transcending time and
place. Ever free, She is revealed in crystal-clear terms by
innumerable Vedic texts, yet remains unclear for gross
intellects. But the first glimpse of Her is enough to make
one understand that She is the highest goal to be attained, the supreme reality known as '*Brahman*.'

Melpattur's lines,[1] issuing from the distant temple, sounded
like dawn's bugle call.

In those days, I never bothered to find out the meaning of
those lines from the *Narayaneeyam*. Even after retiring from

---

1 The first verse from *Narayaneeyam*, in which the poet, Melpattur
Narayana Bhattathiri, sings the glories of the deity of the Guruvayoor
Temple.

long years of teaching, prayer was my only reprieve from sorrows. I was constantly afflicted by diseases, one after another.

I first saw Amma in 1985. Being a devotee of Lord Krishna, I went to meet Her with the sole thought of having His darshan.

My husband and I first saw Her in a house in Koẕhikode. With that first darshan itself, Amma became everything to us — our small family comprising my husband, three children and myself. Thereafter, whenever we had a chance, we would visit Amritapuri, yearning for affection from that embodiment of love. In those days, there were no facilities for accommodating visitors. Two tiny cubicles above the old printing press were the only rooms available for guests. Amma would personally sweep the place and lay out mats for us. Setting aside some food for us from whatever was available, Amma would also nourish us with Her words — spiritual manna. Those were cherished moments with Amma!

We were also blessed with the opportunity to participate in the activities of the Koẕhikode ashram from its very inception. Those days, filled with myriad experiences, were dedicated to Amma. Once a week, many of us would gather to take part in ashram activities. How many opportunities we had to gather for satsang, bhajans and seva activities!

How most of the youth who worked enthusiastically, like members of one family, later became brahmacharis strikes me as amazing. When my own daughter made the same decision,

I could not accept it initially. Then I went to Amritapuri to see my daughter and was stunned — everyone here looked so contented! How could one pluck just one flower from a dazzling white field of roses? Like everyone else I saw, my daughter, too, was full of joy. There were so many children — with beaming faces and foreheads daubed with circles of sandal paste — who addressed me as "Amma." How then could I not see them as my own? I felt secretly proud! My daughter had gained the good fortune with which I had not been blessed. She had chosen the golden path of renunciation and service, leaving behind the path of life I had traveled along, away from the ocean of samsara.

As I progress on the wave of experiences with Amma, I write this with great joy and bliss; with the tranquil heart of a new life given by Amma...

November 7th, 2002: As I was experiencing great difficulty in breathing, I was admitted into a hospital. I had symptoms of cardiac arrest, and was warded immediately in the intensive care unit. Many unfamiliar instruments, tubes and syringes were inserted into my body to save my life. I was treading the fine line between life and death. Truly, I had come face to face with death. Unable to breathe, I started sinking. In that panic, I tore away the mask I had on my face with all the strength I had. A numbness started creeping up my body. I desperately wanted the room's air-conditioning turned off. The fact that I couldn't utter even a word frightened me. I could see my son Murali near me. I looked at him helplessly. Sensing that I was trying to speak, he handed me a pen and a sheet of paper, but I wasn't even able to write. The healthy forget the pitiful plight of a motionless body, remembering it only when confronted by death.

Memories in the form of images surfaced, then faded. *To-morrow is the wedding day of my younger sister's son. My death would inconvenience them all! How lovely was the sari they bought for me! Pity that I won't be able to wear it! The blouse to go along with that sari has not been stitched yet.* Are all unfulfilled desires experienced at the time of death as pain? *No, I have no desire,* I strove to console myself, *save to merge in Amma's holy feet.*

My vision started diminishing. Darkness began spreading. In the sheer effort to breathe, my muscles became tense. Suddenly, I sensed that something had changed. I felt that I had become separate from my body. Yes! I could see everything clearly. My body was lying motionless on a white sheet. Doctors were striving desperately to keep life in it. Outside, relatives and friends were grieving.

I then beheld a new world, different from the one where I had lived out my life. A peace I had never experienced before in life filled me. In that state of rapture, I saw a light. I cannot tell if it was inside or outside me. It was an indescribable experience!

A mighty shower of peace bathed my being. I did not want to return from this new world of peace to the peaceless world.

After some time, memories of Amma began to surface. "O Amma!" I called out spontaneously. Suddenly, I felt as if I had re-entered my body. I could now breathe, though with difficulty. I could also hear my son's voice clearly. Slowly, warmth started spreading throughout my body — it was my second advent into my body! I could now clearly see Amma before me. She was smiling. I have no recollection of what happened thereafter.

I passed one day and night without any awareness of what was happening. When I opened my eyes, I realized that I was still in the I.C.U. but the tubes and syringes that had been inserted into my body had been removed. A great change had taken place in my mind. Worries and diseases had distanced themselves. The form of Amma, the embodiment of Brahman, graced my heart. I felt only joy, no other emotion. It seemed as if I was radiating compassion. I was not able to see anyone as separate from me. I perceived Amma as the divine consciousness pervading all beings.

I badly wanted to let everyone in the world know what I was experiencing. My mind longed to proclaim that the only thing we can offer the world is love, and that we should not lose any opportunity to do so. If only I could convey to everyone the ineffability of that unknown world of peace!

After a few days, I was discharged from the hospital. My mind is at peace even now. There is joy everywhere. Who is to hate whom? We are all members of one family, meant to love each other, to live by sharing love. Express gratitude for what you have, instead of lamenting over what you don't. Isn't that what Amma is teaching us? When I think about how Amma led me into the unfathomable depths of spiritual experience, my heart overflows with contentment. This is the boon I gained from Amma!

(July 2005)

When Amma Says Something
Ashok Nair, Qatar

One lifetime is not enough to understand Amma. I have told myself not to look for the end-point of Infinity.

Our life is like a jigsaw puzzle; experiences come in bits and pieces. When we put them together, we get a bigger picture. What I'm going to narrate is one of the most poignant experiences in my life.

My family was on vacation in India in July or August 2002, and as usual, all of us went to see Amma. During darshan, Amma asked me, "Son, don't you have anything to ask me?" I told Her that I was happy.

We returned home from our vacation in the first week of September. In mid-September, my wife, Suja, caught a fever that lasted three days. We participated in Amma's birthday celebration at my friend's house, and as usual, Suja sang bhajans that day. She was still feeling a little weak, but apart from that, there was nothing unusual.

On the evening of September 30th, she said she was not feeling well and did not know what the problem was. I took her to a doctor, who diagnosed a urinary infection and prescribed some medicines. She took the medicines, but by October 3rd, she was having diarrhea and getting weaker.

On the morning of the 4th, I took her to the Emergency Room in Hamad Hospital, the main government hospital in Doha. The doctors said that the problem was caused by the medication, and they changed it. They also said there was nothing wrong with her. However, her condition deteriorated, and by the evening, she was becoming disoriented, and had difficulty speaking and walking.

I was terrified. I did not know what was happening to Suja. I called my company doctor, who advised me to bring her to a private American hospital the next day. The doctors there ran many tests but still did not see any abnormality. Suja had become very weak and completely disoriented by then. The doctor ordered an MRI scan of her head, which revealed some abnormality. Suja was admitted to Hamad Hospital immediately.

For the next few days, a team of doctors carried out all kinds of tests on her. By October 9th, she started slipping into a coma. I was totally lost, not knowing what to do. I lost my ability to make rational decisions, and was just being bombarded by a wide range of opinions from friends and the people around me. Many, including the hospital staff, advised me to take her to India.

I recalled Amma's words: "Son, don't you have anything to ask me?" I begged Her then to save my wife's life. I wanted to convey a message to Her, but I did not know anyone in Amritapuri. Not only that, Amma was touring Europe then. My friend Murali managed to get in touch with Swami Purnamritananda, who was with Amma in France, and asked him to convey our plight to Amma. On the evening of October 10th, Swami Purnamritananda got back to us with Amma's instructions: "Continue the treatment with the same doctor who is treating Suja."

We can make complex decisions in life if we avail ourselves of the Guru's guidance. I told all my friends that I had decided to continue Suja's treatment in Doha under the care of the doctor who was treating her, and asked them to stop advising me any further. If Suja had been conscious then, I am sure she would have made the same decision.

The next day, I went to see the doctor who was treating Suja. She was in a near coma, and could neither speak nor walk. It was difficult for us to figure out if she recognized any of us. After the doctor examined Suja, I told him that I wished to meet him in private. I learned then that he was Pakistani. Until that day, I had never liked Pakistanis. Not only that, I also believed it was against the (Indian) national spirit to think well about them. I told him that I had no knowledge of medical affairs, and that I needed professional advice from him on what I could do for my wife. I also said that if he felt that I should take her to a particular hospital where she could receive the necessary treatment, I was willing to take her there, no matter where in the world it may be.

He looked down for a while. He then said, "I can understand what you're going through, but what we're doing now is all that can be done for her medically." He then said, "Everything will be okay," and told me to hold out a little longer. He also said that if I wished to take her to any other hospital for social reasons, he was ready to discharge her. However, if I were ready to leave this case to him, he would continue treating Suja as he would his own sister. I told him that I was entrusting Suja's case to him.

That night, the doctor started her on a new medication, and in the next few days, she showed good signs of recovery. She was discharged from the hospital after 14 days. When I took her home, she still could not talk or understand anything. She was not given any new medication, and the dosage of her existing medication ended 10 days after her discharge. She had to undergo rehabilitation therapy, and had to be taught such basic things like putting on clothes and adding numbers.

It may sound incredible if I say that there was never any doubt in my mind that Suja would recover. But it is my faith that when Amma says something, it will happen. Within three months, much to everyone's surprise, she regained 80% of her faculties — she could talk, walk, sing and drive again. Now, almost six years later, she has recovered almost 99%.

On one of the follow-up visits, the doctor told me that even after two years, he could clearly remember the day I had walked into his room to speak to him. He admitted that he had lied to me when he said that everything was going to be fine. He showed me the medical file; in it, he had written that day: "The patient is not responding to any medication, and her condition is getting worse." He then said that he had never expected her to recover. When Suja thanked him for his help, he said, "I did not do anything to you. You cured yourself." He also told us that she was the strangest patient he had treated. He asked me if I had taken Suja to see any other doctor while on vacation or for a second opinion. I told him that I had not because our Guru had told us to continue Suja's treatment with him. Suja showed him the ring she was wearing; it had Amma's picture on it. Very innocently, the doctor told us to convey his appreciation to our Guru for the faith She had shown in him.

When Suja was admitted to the hospital, her case had actually been referred to another doctor, but 'by mistake,' an attendant had kept the file on the table of the doctor who ended up treating her. The doctor told me that when he looked at the case, he had found it interesting, and that is why he had taken it up.

On April 17th, 2005, the doctor closed her file, and told her that there was no need for further checkups.

When Suja recovered fully, she told me that she had black-outs only during the first few days after being admitted, and that after that, she used to see and recognize all of us, but it was always dreamlike. There was an Arabic woman attendant who used to come to see Suja every night, and she would tell Suja and the people sitting by her side that Suja was going to be fine. This woman wore a *burka*, the traditional Arab dress, and only her eyes would be visible. Most of the women who stayed with Suja at night (as it was a women's ward, only women were permitted to stay with patients) were scared of her appearance. However, Suja used to eagerly wait for her to come everyday because she used to see Amma in her.

Over the course of Suja's illness and subsequent recovery, I learned to appreciate the value of friendship. I realized that man is a helpless creature, who is not in control of his destiny. However, sincere effort and prayer always draws God's grace.

Our lives are a gift from Amma, and I surrender my life at the sacred feet of my Guru.

(December 2010)

Meeting the Mata
Aftab Ahmed, India

It was early September 2004. I was minding my shop at Varkala one evening when a good friend came by for tea. He wanted to go to Amritapuri, but did not know the way. I had heard about the Mata but was not interested, being naturally cautious and having found a comfortable Zen meditation center, where I went a couple of times a year. I was married with two beautiful children, and my health and business were good. My father had passed away five years ago, and I had largely gotten over the grief, but my mother was not well. She had suffered some brain damage a decade earlier and would suddenly get violent or weep for no reason. This was frightening the children and my wife. With vague misgivings but thinking a drive through Kerala would be nice, I offered to drop my friend at the ashram the next day, have a look around and then return.

We reached the ashram at about three in the afternoon. Music filled the air. As we stepped through the gateway, something moved in my chest. "It must be the music," I thought, as we reached the main hall where darshan was going on. There amidst the thronging masses, I beheld a still white figure much like an idol worshipped in a temple. My friend was trying to get into the darshan line, without success, nor could he get information about how to get into the line. Frustrated, he crossed the hall to the other side. I followed him. While crossing, I looked at the figure again, closer this time, and saw a serious, powerful countenance in a bluish hue; I had to look away. Meanwhile, my friend had no success and was getting desperate. To calm him down, I suggested a sandwich and coffee at the café nearby. As he was planning to stay a few days, I told him he would eventually get into the darshan line.

As we munched the food slowly, I scanned the crowd, and saw boards with large numbers indicating darshan token numbers. I was trying to figure out if the whole thing was a scam when a former customer walked by. I hailed him, to his surprise, and asked him if he knew how to get into the line. "You cannot get into the line, you need to get a token early in the morning," he said. "But I can help you get in line if you wish," he said to my friend.

"In that case, I would like to come, too," I said abruptly, taken aback at my own forwardness.

He took us up to the stage while I kept commenting to myself about the teeming crowd and how servile they seemed. Standing at the corner of the stage, I felt everyone was making a big fuss about this white-clad figure. I, too, knew how to meditate. Why should they be so obsequious and emotional? I reached a turn in the line from where I could see Her clearly. A sparkling mist seemed to surround Her. I thought it must be the humidity and lights. Then, suddenly, I started weeping. From hidden depths, an unknown grief welled up, shaking me with its causeless immediacy. I went to the corner of the stage and wept my heart out against the wall, trying to hide from people. A part of me was shocked at this. I was not grieving for my father. After a few minutes, I managed to collect myself and stood in line. "Now you must behave," I told myself. How to behave? How does one behave near a saint? They respectfully ask the saint for help to solve some problem. What was my problem? My mother. I resolved to say just this to Her and then leave without further drama.

When my turn came, I was perplexed but the attendant gently laid my head on Her shoulder, and for a while my mind went blank. In Tamil, She whispered, "My dearest son, my dearest son." It sounded far away, from across the cosmos. As I stood up, I tried to tell Her my problem but was whisked away quickly. Obediently returning to the corner, I waited for my friend to finish his darshan. After a few minutes, the attendant looked directly at me across the stage and gestured for me to sit down. It is someone else I thought, but he repeated the gesture and I sat down. Almost immediately, someone else asked me to move a bit to make space. A little later, someone else did the same. Then another got up in front and another asked me to move again. In this manner, within the span of a few minutes, I ended up right next to Her. Perhaps I can ask Her this time, I thought. She was talking, joking and laughing like a young girl, and engrossed in play with friends. I asked a man nearby, also clad in white, if She knew Tamil. When he said yes, I tried to get a word in edgeways but could not. Her banter and jolly laughter continued, such a contrast to the serious demeanor when I first saw Her face. Seeing my predicament, the man said, "Don't worry. She knows your problem without your having to say anything." This, my mind did not agree with, but She suddenly turned around to a man next to me and said loudly in Tamil "Summa irru!" ("Keep still!"). Though not directed at me, the remark hit home. I stopped trying to say anything and sat quietly for a while. Then bowing down respectfully, I left.

Outside, I said goodbye to my friend. I was in a dazed peace. Something had happened and I did not know what. I asked him to keep my visit here private. I needed time to understand this.

That night, at my temporary lodgings at Varkala, I sat to meditate for a while before sleeping. But I could not sleep. I meditated again, and again tried to sleep, but to no avail. I got up and wandered in the silence of the unfamiliar house when I saw an altar to Her, left in disarray by the previous occupant. I immediately cleaned it up and, although a Muslim, burned the incense nearby, trying to be humble. "I am sin and sinner. Even though my will is weak, I will do everything You ask of me." I wept internally to Her.

Sleep did not come and the battle continued until dawn, when the muezzin from a nearby mosque called for morning prayers. "God is great, God is great, there is no God but God" — a beautiful call, a relief from the dark silence. I slept for an hour or so, bathed and went to my shop, trying to act normal. At nights, I still couldn't sleep, and this went on for the next three days. Finally, on the third day, unable to take it anymore and feeling I would die at any moment, I left for home to Kodaikanal to be with my wife and children.

My mother was her usual sullen self. I did not speak to her. For two nights, I heard her weeping in her room in the middle of the night, but as she seemed safe, I did not intrude. The transformation took place on the third day. Coming out of her room and bumping into my son, her face was wreathed in the most beautiful smile. Later, when my daughter returned home from school, my mother was equally friendly and engaging. Within the day, they were the best of friends, spending time in her room playing and laughing, with no trace of the past. After years of treatments that did not work, how had this happened? I had done nothing.

"Don't worry. She knows your problem without your having to say anything." Those words came back to me. I understood and was humbled.

Since this incident, life has changed for the better. Although my mother still has mood swings, they are mild and nothing like before. The children are growing up well and there is harmony at home.

There are numerous other incidents that have made me understand better what the spirit is and shown up both my arrogant ignorance as well as the unconditional mercy of the Satguru. Words such as faith, love, respect and devotion are too weak to express my feelings. The scriptures declare, "Of all the blessings obtained in life, none is greater than association with a Sage."

May everyone gain this blessing. May none suffer. *Lokah samastah sukhino bhavantu* (May all beings everywhere be happy).

(July 2011)

Blessed

Journey

Maverick
Sugunanandan-acchan,[1] India

I had a Guru before Amma. He was my *Kathakali*[2] teacher. I used to watch Kathakali performances and felt there was something special about them — the crown, the costumes and the dance itself. Apart from that, I didn't have any special knowledge about Kathakali or about how one went about acquiring that knowledge. When I was in fifth grade, I felt I should study Kathakali.

So, I started training under my Guru, and eventually made my début in a temple. In those days, Kathakali was the main performing art in temples. There would sometimes be four-day festivals, during which four Kathakali performances would be presented, one each day.

Once, my teacher's Kathakali troupe was invited to perform in a place called Trikunnapuzha. We presented the story of 'Duryodhana-vadha,' the slaying of Duryodhana.[3] It was the fourth day of the performance. I was playing Lord Krishna. The actor playing the Lord had to be present from the very begin-

....

1 The author, Amma's father, gave this talk in Amritapuri on Guru Purnima on July 18th, 2008. 'Acchan' means 'father,' in Malayalam. 'Accha' is the vocative form. Sugunanandan-acchan was often called 'Sugunacchan.'
2 A form of dance-drama native to Kerala.

ning until the end, when Duryodhana is killed. I could not step out of my costume or remove my crown even for a minute.

In the final part of the dance, Bhima hits Duryodhana repeatedly. However, Bhima doesn't know where Duryodhana's weak spot is. Only if Bhima hits him there can he kill him. Every time Bhima hits him, Duryodhana falls down, only to get up again the next moment. Finally, Bhima becomes exhausted. He calls out prayerfully to Lord Krishna, "O Lord!"

Bhima's prayer takes the form of a long song. As soon as the song starts, Lord Krishna has to appear on stage; that was my cue. However, I had fallen asleep in the dressing room, which was right next to the stage. It had been a long night and was almost dawn! I woke up after the song had started and ran toward the stage. In those days, one had to perform on a pedestal. When I tried to mount it, I slipped. My Guru, who was standing nearby, thumped me hard in the back. Enraged, I mounted the pedestal.

As I stood there, simmering with anger, I thought, "I've been performing until dawn, and he hits me on the back! I should just throw all this away! I don't need any of this!"

----

3 Duryodhana, a character from the *Mahabharata*, was the leader of the unrighteous Kaurava clan. He had earlier won a boon that would make every inch of his body, save his thigh, invulnerable to all attacks.

As I stood holding the mace and discus, I was literally quivering with rage; the blow on my back had caused me to shake with anger. In the play, the actor playing Krishna has to quiver for a long time until Duryodhana dies. Seeing my performance, my Guru was extremely pleased. He wondered, "How did he ever manage that!"

Anger towards my Guru became the cause of his pleasure. Actually, it wasn't me dancing, but the anger. All those who saw me were very impressed with my performance. They complemented me, saying how amazing it was that I could perform so admirably even after so many hours. When I returned to the dressing room, my Guru lifted me, placed me on his lap, and kissed me over and over again, so pleased was he by my performance! I wasn't so mad with him anymore. I felt very happy.

Whatever the Guru says or does is for the disciple's own good; that's the greatness of the Guru. If my Guru hadn't done what he did, I wouldn't have performed so well. Truly, the Guru's every deed takes us higher and higher in spiritual life.

~

One morning, Damayanti-amma[4] told me, "I had a dream."

"What?" I asked.

---

4 Amma's mother.

"I saw myself giving birth to Lord Krishna, holding Him in my lap, and breastfeeding Him."

"Nothing surprising about that!" I said. "You worship God 24 hours a day. That's why you see Him in your dreams. I don't see Him, do I? I see other things in my dreams — all kinds of petty businessman and other people!"

A few days later, Damayanti-amma told me, "I saw a big light, which seemed to be coming towards me. Then suddenly, I didn't see it anymore."

Damayanti-amma became pregnant after seeing this light. I wasn't with her when she gave birth; no one was. We had a small roadside provision store selling rice, chili and other basic food items. Damayanti-amma worked there. She went to the shop even on the day of Amma's birth. Suddenly, she left the shop and returned to the kalari, and gave birth to Amma in this house. No one else was present.

For some reason, an old woman from the neighboring house came by. The newborn baby wasn't moving or making any sound. Damayanti-amma and the old woman were worried. Three of our children had already died, one before Kasturi, and the two who came after her. The old woman lifted the child and looked at it. After a few moments, she said, "It's alive!" She bathed the child. After the bath, the woman said, "It's smiling!" Damayanti-amma felt relieved.

Once, when I returned home from work, Damayanti-amma was in the kitchen. Amma was about four or five months old at that time. She was lying in the crib and wailing. I picked Her up and started singing a lullaby to stop Her crying. She peed and pooped all over me! I am talking about your Guru here! I put Her back in the crib and told Damayanti-amma, "Damayanti, I can't handle her anymore."

Recently, when Damayanti-amma and I dropped by Amma's room, She said, "Accha, you threw me into the crib when I pooped, didn't you?"

At first, I had no idea what She was talking about. Then I remembered that incident. Sometimes, we wonder, how does She remember all these things? We've had many experiences like these.

Damayanti-amma would get up at four in the morning, pluck flowers, and do a puja in the kalari. As I wasn't interested in pujas, I would continue sleeping. Amma would also wake up early to help Damayanti-amma by bringing flowers, and then She would also take part in the puja. My other children would be sleeping. Amma wasn't like them.

She also read spiritual literature. She started reading the *Bhagavatam* all by Herself. I told Damayanti-amma, "You read the *Ramayana*[5] and *Bhagavatam* with Her, creating bhakti in

5 An epic on the life of Lord Rama, one of the incarnations of Lord Vishnu.

that girl. Let her study. She should study at least until the 10th grade."

Damayanti-amma protested, "I never wake her up. She wakes up on her own and comes to help me."

In the morning, all the children, including Amma, would go to school, but Amma would reach only after the school bell had rung. She was late for school every day. Her teachers, who knew me, asked, "Sugunananda, why is your daughter always late for school? It has become habitual!"

When I asked Amma why, She didn't say anything. The children who went to school with Her told me, "She goes to the homes of poor people. If they are sick, she caresses them. She serves them food. If she has anything with her, she gives it to them. That's why she's always late."

I told Her, "Don't do this anymore," but it was no use. She continued in Her ways. Finally, the school dismissed Her. She had passed fourth grade. I tried to enlist Her in a school in Kollam, but failed. So, Amma stayed at home and did all the housework.

She did everything for Damayanti-amma. She visited every house in the vicinity to collect anything they would give — money, rice, even tapioca peels, which are fodder for cows. Then She went to the houses where people were suffering, and gave those things to them. Sometimes, we would be left with no money to buy rice even. I would spank Her, but She continued helping the poor and needy, undeterred.

Damayanti-amma's parents lived alone; everyone else had moved out. Amma declared, "I'll go there and help them!" She did all the work there. Her grandparents had plenty of rice-paddy, which they stored in a big wooden case. Amma quietly took some to give the poor neighbors. When the grandparents found out, they sent Amma packing, telling us not to send Her anywhere else!

Later, while visiting Damayanti-amma's elder sister, Amma told her, "I shall help you." There, every time the coconuts were plucked, Amma would take many of them and give them to the poor neighbors.

Amma thus worked in various houses. Her only motivation was to help the poor. Whatever She received, She gave to others.

Once, I bought a pair of earrings for Amma. She wore them for only a week. The next week, I asked Her, "Where are the earrings?"

At first She said, "I kept them somewhere," and then became evasive. She wouldn't tell me the truth. I thought to myself, "This isn't right." I took a stick and beat Her until Her legs bled. Then She admitted the truth. "There's an old woman in a neighboring house. She hasn't eaten anything for the last three days. I gave her my earrings."

If any beggar stopped outside our house, and if his or her clothes were tattered, Amma would give away our clothes without our knowledge to the beggar. Do you know how we found out? The beggar's dirty clothes would be on our hangers! Because of this, She was often spanked during Her childhood.

Recently, someone who had read Amma's biography came to me and asked, "Are you Acchan?"

I politely replied, "Yes, I am."

He said, "How could you have been so cruel?"

"What do you mean?" I asked.

"Didn't you beat Amma many times? Why did you do that?"

I remonstrated, "Amma didn't tell us She was divine! Of course, I now realize what I did was wrong." I then said, "Can I ask you something? Didn't Yashoda tie Lord Krishna up and hit Him? Why don't you object to that? Didn't Lord Rama's stepmother banish Him to the forest? Wasn't that wrong also? We also erred, just like them. Like them, we, too, didn't know Amma was God incarnate."

When Amma was around 16 or 17, we considered many marriage proposals for Her. In the end, we settled upon one man. When he came here to see Amma, She rushed towards him with a five-foot pestle, intending to clobber him! We never saw him again. We felt deeply ashamed.

I asked Amma, "How could you do that? He came at our invitation, didn't he?"

Amma retorted, "You can arrange marriages for your other children, not for me. Don't even think about it!"

Thereafter, we stopped trying. What if Amma were to chase away the next man that came also?

~

Every day, after sunset, our daughter would go to some solitary spot to meditate. As there was no ashram in this area then, we didn't know anything about meditation or japa. She would murmur something or the other that we didn't understand. Thinking that She was muttering gibberish, I would grab Her hands to take Her home.

There was a latrine by the backwaters. Sometimes, Amma would go there and start muttering to Herself. It was a private place, and no one would see Her going there. Even if they did, Amma would continue mumbling.

She would also gaze at the pictures of deities, which Damayanti-amma had hung on the wall, and spend a long time talking to them. We saw many instances of such odd behavior in Amma. We never understood what She was doing. At that time, there was nobody to tell us about sadhana. Amma didn't tell us about it either.

Damayanti-amma was very particular that girls should not talk loudly. She would say the ceiling shouldn't hear what they say. But Amma always spoke loudly!

~

Amma's smile and dance during Krishna Bhava created an atmosphere of divine joy that many people relished. The villagers, however, opposed the Krishna Bhava and created many problems for us. They lodged a case against us with the police. Even our own relatives turned against us. They said, "Why is she prancing around like this?"

Then Devi Bhava began. Those who said that Krishna Bhava was shameful alleged that Devi Bhava was fraudulent. Some taunted us, saying, "If you don't have money to pay for her dowry and marriage expenses, we can lend you some!"

Amma would start the Devi Bhava by dancing, and what an awesome sight that was! I don't know who gave Her that huge sword and trident; just seeing them was frightening enough! Amma would wield them both and dance wildly in the kalari for three or four hours. The floor, which was paved with strong concrete, would crack! That's how powerful Amma's dance was!

I found the whole thing extremely distressing. As far as I was concerned, my daughter was creating a scene in public.

After Devi Bhava, there would be no movement in Amma's body at all for quite some time. This frightened me. People would sprinkle water on Her body to rouse Her. One day, I told Her, "Look, if you're Devi, go to Kodungullur or Mandakkadu.[6] Leave my daughter alone!"

Amma retorted, "What you call your daughter will just collapse and die. What will you do with that daughter of yours? You will have to cremate her! Therefore, I'm not your daughter. The *Atma* (Self) comes from God. You have a right only to the body."

Angrily, I snapped, "Don't argue with me!"

The next day, during Devi Bhava, I sullenly stayed away. After some time, I heard people shouting, "She has collapsed! She has died! She's not breathing! We poured a little water into Her mouth, but it's not going inside!" People started wailing loudly and hitting their chests piteously.

When I arrived on the scene, I saw Amma's lifeless body. Three hours passed. Throwing myself prostrate before Amma, I hugged Her body and cried, "O my Amma, I will never speak that way again! I only did so because I considered You my daughter." Even now, when I recall that scene, I cannot bear it.

---

6 Temples dedicated to Devi (the Goddess) in Central and North Kerala respectively.

After that, we saw some movement in Her body; She came back to life. Ever since then, I haven't said anything about Her being my daughter to Amma; I haven't even had the guts to think like that! That experience gave us more faith in Amma's divinity.

Back then, I didn't have total faith in Amma's divinity. One day, She called me and said, "Do not doubt. There's going to be much more here than what you're seeing now..."

Amma then spoke about how the number of devotees was going to increase exponentially. I didn't believe Her then.

Many people continued coming here. I would ask some, "Where are you from?"

"Vavakkavu."

"Have you come here before?"

"We come for every Bhava darshan."

"Why?"

"After coming here, so many good things have happened to us."

Once, a woman told me, "I've been married for 10 years, but hadn't conceived. This baby here came about after we received Amma's blessings."

I kept hearing stories like this. Slowly, I began to believe.

Today, many people ask me, "Accha, Amma has become world-famous. When you see all this, do you ever become egoistic?"

I say, "Not at all. I'm an ordinary person. The person behind all this is someone else. I feel great joy seeing all this. Damayanti-amma and I consider it our great fortune to have been witness to this unique divine drama. But we take no credit for anything."

~

I once asked Amma, "You build houses for so many people. Why don't You build one for me?"

"Why do you need so many rooms?" Amma asked. "You don't need them!" She instructed the brahmachari in charge of the ashram accounts, "Don't ever give even a loan to Acchan!"

So, whenever I ask him for a loan, he says, "We'll think about it." Sometimes, he says, "I'll ask Amma."

After a few days, when I ask him, "Have you asked Amma?" he doesn't say anything. I know he wouldn't have asked Amma, because She has already instructed him not to give me anything.

So, now, I live next to the vegetable shop! If someone asks, "Where is Acchan?" people here say, "Next to the vegetable shop." Seriously, my only desire now is to live by my own earnings. Even at this age, I make boats. I don't take a single *paisa* from anyone.

Sometimes, when I feel like seeing Amma, I go to Her room. As soon as I arrive, Amma asks, "Why did you come? What do you want to tell me? Go away! I've so many matters to attend to!"

Sometimes, She says, "When Acchan comes, I can't get any work done!" I then say good-bye and leave!

Once, I had a ring. It was too tight. I approached Amma and said, "I want another ring instead of this one."

Amma said, "Why would an old man like you need a ring? Call on God! He is the only true friend!"

I kept quiet. Then Amma said, "Lakshmi,[7] take that ring from him."

She took the ring. I thought I would get another one, but Lakshmi just took the ring and left! Amma then said, "There's no ring here. Please leave!"

I felt terribly embarrassed. When I returned home, Damayanti-amma asked me, "Where's your ring, Accha?"

I replied, "I lost what I had and what I was expecting." I then told her what had happened.

Damayanti-amma said, "How shameful! Why did you bother going to all this trouble?"

Four days after this incident, Damayanti-amma and I were sitting in front of the house. Radhamani was cleaning the

----

7 Bri. Lakshmi is Amma's personal attendant.

courtyard. At 4:10 p.m. sharp, an eagle came out of nowhere, swooped down and dropped something. Radhamani noticed it and said, "The eagle dropped something." I told her to take it. It was a watch and a ring; both fit me perfectly!

I thought about this. Ordinarily, an eagle will pick up only useless scrap. It won't carry such things for a long distance. Moreover, there were many other workers standing around that area, but it dropped the items right before us. Not only that, the eagle then flew up to a coconut tree and remained there until we had picked up those items!

I immediately went to the telephone room and told Br. Raju, "Call Amma right now."

He asked, "What's the matter, Accha?"

"Just call Amma!"

He dialed the number and gave me the phone. I told Amma, "Why did you send those things through the eagle? I could have come personally to collect them."

Amma said, "What?"

I said, "I could've taken those items from you. You needn't have sent them through the eagle!"

Amma kept mum! She hasn't said a single word about the ring until now. She hasn't even asked to see it.

I've kept the ring in my puja room. Some of you have seen it. Some people may not believe such a thing took place; that's why I've kept it in the puja room. All those who have seen it say they haven't seen a ring like that before.

There have been many such miracles in our lives.

(October 2008)

Over Gleaming Embers
Kasturibai, India

People show me respect because of my mother, who is rich in spiritual merit, and my younger sister, the very Goddess of the Universe. My younger sister bravely trod the most arduous path, strewn with gleaming embers, as it were. She, who glowed like a lamp in our tiny village, is now the beacon-light for millions all over the world. My kid sister, Sri Mata Amritanandamayi Devi, cannot be adequately described by words nor grasped by emotion.

Ours was a below-middle-class fisher family. My father Sugunacchan ran a few small businesses. My mother, Damayantiamma was the very personification of devotion. The villagers dubbed her 'Pattatti-amma' (Brahmin lady) on account of her piety and adherence to orthodox religious practices. She had 11 children. I was the second child. My older sister, Ratnambika, died when she was four-and-a-half years old. I was two-and-a-half then. Right after me came Subhagan. After him came a baby boy, who passed away in the month of *Tulam* (October – November), 53 days after he was born.

Eleven months later, in *Kanni* (September), my mother gave birth to Sri Mata Amritanandamayi Devi. Sudhamani, as She was named, incarnated on a *Kartika* (the third constellation, Pleiades) day, at 8:30 a.m. A memory now dawns clearly in my mind — the legs of the baby were bent at the knees; it was as if She were seated in the lotus posture. I now realize this truth, which the four-year-old I was at that time could not understand. Every stage of Her physical growth was stupendous. She did not turn over to crawl; She just stood up. Before She could even sit up properly, she was already trying to toddle. We noticed all these signs but lacked the wisdom to understand their import.

Whenever I see Amma — who embraces all who come before Her, takes on their pains, and whom countless people worship — I feel a secret happiness within. I have carried this Amma in my arms. I have rocked Her to sleep on my shoulder. I have walked to Kuzhittura Fisheries School, holding the hand of Subhagan, who has since died, with one hand, and Sudhamani's hand with the other.

When it came to studies, She was extraordinarily brilliant. As students, Subhagan and I would buy sweets with the coins our father or uncles gave us. But I never saw Amma do that. In fact, She would give the money to those who were sad. Whatever Amma's received was for the happiness of others, whereas ours were for our own pleasure. Even at that young age, Amma sacrificed Her own happiness for the sake of others.

Amma is dark-skinned whereas I am more light-skinned. Nevertheless, She never complained about it or whined about not being more fair-skinned. I now see that even then, there was no place for such thoughts in Her mind. Not only that, Amma never showed any partiality for bright or shiny clothes.

As the eldest child, I occupied a special position in the family. But, today, Amma enjoys pride of place in the hearts of many.

Amma started getting severe stomach pains while in fourth grade. It would start shortly after She reached school. The teacher would send Her home. Amma would be escorted home by Aisha, daughter of Sugunacchan's sister. My brother and I never knew about these episodes.

In those days, Damayanti-amma was in poor health. I now feel that Amma left school so that She could take on Her mother's workload. As soon as She reached home, Amma would immerse Herself in household chores, without saying a word about Her stomach pains. From that tender age onwards, Amma took on the burden of all the housework.

After Amma stopped going to school, She took charge of the kitchen. As we scurried to get ready for school, She would enthusiastically prepare our meals and pack them for us. She would then stand watching from the doorway as we walked to school. Time has proven how much more exalted is the wisdom Amma attained compared with the knowledge we gained from school and college. Today, Amma is Guru to the ignorant and wise alike.

I also remember some of the more curious incidents that took place in those days. As we used to own a cow, we children had to go out to pluck grass. In this, Amma was highly skilled. She would collect twice as much grass as we did, and in half the time. Then She would disappear. We would eventually find Her sitting alone with eyes closed; Amma was communing with God. Not realizing this, we continued to find fault with Her.

On auspicious days, our family would serve food to the poor from the lower castes. We never let them enter the house, but served them food in the front yard. This was the social custom in those days; people from higher castes would not even go near those of lower castes. We would give them an earthen pot full of rice porridge as well as a towel and some oil. In the twinkling of an eye, Amma would appear among the people who were sitting far away and drinking porridge, and start drinking porridge from their plates. Because of this, quite a few people from our village and within our caste started speaking derisively about us. Amma would also not hesitate to cuddle and kiss little children who were dirty. She never noticed the dirt on the external body. Whenever anyone expressed any sorrow, Amma gave them money from our house.

In those days, we sisters never adorned ourselves with bangles or marks on our foreheads because our mother never approved of such behavior. Damayanti-amma raised her four daughters with utmost strictness. We had to wake up at four a.m. If we did not, she would pour water over our heads. There were many occasions when my sisters and I would wake up drenched, but never Amma. She always woke up in time.

Whenever we had a tug-of-war with the sheet or blanket, Amma would remain aloof. Not only that, She would relinquish Her share of the sheet as well. But after everyone had fallen asleep, the blanket would be Hers!

When it came to food, Amma was an angel. She would give Her share of the food to others to ward off their hunger pangs. She used to take special delight in filling our stomachs.

Amma was especially fond of Satheesh, our younger brother. This made me jealous. There was a 10-year gap between the two. From his infancy, Amma looked after him, like a hen protecting its chick under its wings. He had asthma from a tender age. Whenever he fell sick, Amma would take him across the backwaters to the Vallickavu Government Hospital. She would stand in line, buy medicines and then return home with him. Today, the hospitals that She runs, including AIMS Hospital, are giving a new lease on life to hundreds of thousands of patients. Then as now, the sick and those suffering from pain enjoy Her special grace.

Amma started going for tailoring classes while I was studying in the Industrial Training Institute (ITI) in Karunagapally. She was 15 then. Even though She first started lessons in a house in Clappana, She continued them at the Clappana Chapel. Amma picked up the fundamentals of tailoring quickly. Seeing how well She applied what She had learned, we were amazed. She soon became accomplished in hand sewing, embroidery and machine stitching. Soon, She began getting orders from villagers. She would take cloth to the church, where She would stitch skirts, shirts and petticoats. If She received any money for these, She would hand it over to Damayanti-amma.

When Amma was about 17, She went to a neighboring house during a reading of the *Bhagavatam* there. That was when She revealed Her divinity. This happened during the month of *Kumbham* (February – March) on the day of *Ketta* (18th lunar asterism, Antares). When Amma showed some *mudra* (a hand gesture of mystic import), some of those present declared that She was an incarnation of God. One of them asked if She could show proof of Her divinity. I did not see all this.

After this incident, for some days, Amma did not speak much to us but started spending more time in meditation. This continued until the next Ketta day, the following month. That day, Amma again went to the neighboring house during the prayers and reading of the *Bhagavatam*. I followed Her, unable to contain my curiosity. There was another reason for this: all that talk about Amma and Her own aloofness hurt me. That day, Amma transmuted the water in a tumbler that the people of the house presented Her into *panchamritam* (a sweet pudding made from five ingredients). I witnessed this incident with my own eyes. After distributing the panchamritam as prasad to all those gathered there, Amma left. Feeling quite distressed by this whole thing, I followed Her silently.

I felt bad that my younger sister, who had come of age, was doing all this, because in our culture, women, especially younger and unmarried girls are expected to be meek and subservient. However, I also sensed that there was some divine power in Her. As a student of electronics, I should have been inclined towards rationalism, but when I reflected upon this matter calmly, a voice within told me that I — who was senior to Amma in age, who prided herself upon her superior education, and who was fair-skinned — could never do what Amma was doing. That was when I started having faith in Amma's divine power. *"Vishvasam tannenne rakshikku, jagadambe..."* ("O Mother of the Universe, bestow faith on me, and thus save me...") — this prayer from Amma became a blessing in my life.

After this phenomenal event, many people started coming to see Amma. She would sing bhajans with them. After bhajans, She would give Krishna Bhava darshan, during which She would dispense holy ash and sacred water to the devotees. She cured the diseases of many devotees, who would return. It was only when they told us about how Amma had healed them out of Her compassion that we learned about it.

In those days, Krishna Bhava darshans would take place on Sunday, Tuesday, Thursday and Friday. Amma would light a lamp in front of what is the kalari in the ashram today, and start giving darshan. It was the cowshed in our house that later became the kalari. We stood watching as those whose illnesses had been cured, and whose sorrow had been mitigated, presented Her with silk clothes, a crown and a trident. My sister, who used to move about in a blouse and skirt, became their beloved deity.

Once, the lamp that had been lit for the Bhava darshan started dying out as there was no more oil left. Gazing at the wick, Amma made a gesture denoting benediction. The lamp continued burning brightly until the Bhava darshan ended, even though there wasn't even a drop of oil left. This incident strengthened my faith in Amma's divine power. She would not speak about the changes that took place in Her during Bhava darshan. Those were the days when even Her own father and siblings looked upon Her suspiciously. But during Bhava darshan, Harshan (our cousin) and Unni (now Swami Tureeyamritananda) would remain by Her side.

Sugunacchan was adamant that those who came for Bhava darshan should leave the premises as soon as darshan ended. I now realize how much anxiety the change in his daughter's demeanor during Bhava darshans and the sight of devotees flocking to see Her must have caused him. As a father of daughters, Sugunacchan also experienced much consternation and sorrow owing to the arrival of brahmacharis. Once, when

I served Br. Sri (now Swami Purnamritananda) some porridge after bhajans, Sugunacchan rebuked me sharply.

Back then, on Sundays, my friends and I would gather flowers to make garlands. We would then place the garlands around Amma's neck, as She stood in Krishna Bhava. At that time, Amma would repeat all that we had said about Her while collecting the flowers and weaving the garlands.

There used to be only one bus to Vallickavu Junction. People from afar would alight there and take a boat cross the backwaters in order to get Amma's darshan. If anyone asked where they were going, they would say they were going to see 'Vallickavil-amma' ('Amma from Vallickavu'). So, it was the devotees from outside who started calling Her 'Vallickavil-amma.'

Once, when devotees came, a heavy downpour started. There wasn't even enough standing room for everyone in the kalari. Lo, it started pouring all around the kalari and Amma's house, skirting just these two places!

Whenever I alighted at the Vallickavu bus stop after returning from classes, many used to jeer and yell, "Krishna! Krishna!" Holding back tears, I would reach the jetty. After taking the boat across and reaching Amma's presence, all my anguish would dissolve.

Some people started expressing their antagonism towards Amma and the Bhava darshans. Although the number of antagonists was small, their behavior upset my father greatly. During that period, my mind began entertaining many thoughts: What if Amma and I ran away to some far-off place? Or, what if the two of us committed suicide together? I was tutoring some children then, and had saved a small sum of money. One day, I went to Amma and told Her, "I have saved some money from the tutoring. With that money, we can construct an ashram."

When She heard this, Amma started laughing. Actually, all I had in mind was a thatched hut. Amma still teases me about this occasionally: "Aren't you the darling daughter who said she would construct an ashram for me by tutoring?" She would relate this to the swamis, too.

The villagers and relatives who opposed Amma then revere, love and worship Her now. That's enough. Amma blessed those who came to Her. Thus, their lives became elevated.

Amma insisted that Her sisters' weddings be expedited. The first marriage to take place was Sugunamma's. After that was my marriage, in 1980. Sajani's was conducted in 1981. As soon as all the girls in the family were married off, Amma registered the ashram. After my marriage, Sugunacchan donated 10 *cents* (0.1 acres) of land to the ashram. That's when the ashram came into being. The first ashram residents built huts and started staying in them.

Once, Amma told them to build new huts. Two days after the huts had been constructed, new brahmacharis arrived. Amma could foresee their arrival.

After marriage, I was sent to Cheriyazhikkal. Even so, I would come daily to see Amma. One day, when I went to see Her, Amma touched my stomach and chanted, "Shiva! Shiva!" Weeks later, I learned that I was pregnant, but Amma's eye of wisdom had already seen it. Later, She named my baby 'Shivan.'

Amma initiated humanitarian projects right from the time of the ashram's inception. She offered help to those who could not afford to get married or build their own houses. In 1995 or 1996, Amma launched *Amritakuteeram*, the project to build homes for the destitute homeless. Amma's birthday celebrations became the launching pad for humanitarian initiatives. Soon after Amma launched Amritakuteeram, She started *Amritanidhi*, a pension scheme for the destitute. Then, every birthday, She would conduct mass marriages. During Amma's 50th birthday celebrations, She conducted 108 weddings. Thus, owing to Amma's compassion, many people, who would otherwise not have been able to afford it, have been able to get married. Amma even secured jobs for many of them thereafter. All these are ample proof that Amma has provided sufficient nourishment for families to grow and flourish.

All of us have our whims and fancies. I don't have too many. Even before my son was born, Amma had called out to him and named him. That son is now married and has children. I am a grandmother! While dandling my grandchildren on my lap, I have but one story to tell them: the story of the Idamannel family and of my sister, Amma. My prayer is that they walk the righteous path, and I have the faith that Amma will bless them so that they can overcome the obstacles they encounter in their journey through life, just as She has blessed all our family and continues to bless the whole world.

(December 2011)

Blessed Journey

Satheesh Idamannel, India

I was one among eight children in the Idamannel family, born after Sudhamani, now known the world over as 'Amma.' I remember Her engaged in looking after the household even at a tender age, studying and, on top of it all, taking care of the helpless and comforting them. I do not know when She found respite from these hectic activities. Even today, there is not a moment when Amma is not engaged in action — darshan, service projects, and ministering to Her children. But now I know that Amma is at peace even amidst all these activities.

Most of my childhood memories are related to my illness. I was asthmatic from a very young age. During the monsoon season, the illness would become more pronounced. If I contracted some other disease, the asthma would also make its appearance, like a regular guest, making things even worse. Illness and helplessness were my lot. When I voiced my fears, others would not understand. The elders would try to help me based on the meaning they attributed to my cries. But Amma was not like that. She knew my mind. For that reason, my love for Amma grew and I became close to Her. Without my telling Her, She would understand my physical and mental sufferings and act accordingly.

Once, during a rainy season, my breathing difficulties became particularly severe. The elders in my family made me lie down and put thick coverings over me before going about their tasks. Loneliness augmented the intensity of my suffering. Soon, high fever and exhaustion set in, and before long, I became unconscious.

Suddenly, Amma appeared from nowhere, came close to me, roused me from my unconsciousness and consoled me. She then carried me on Her shoulder and went out. In those days, there were no vehicles connecting our village — which was surrounded by the sea and backwaters — to the outside world. After crossing the backwaters in a boat, Amma started walking briskly to the government hospital, carrying me on Her shoulder. She virtually ran the entire distance. I still remember, with senses dimmed and only half conscious in the heat of the fever, how I clung on to Amma, putting my arms around Her neck. At the hospital, I was given medicines and temporarily relieved from suffering.

When I became slightly better, it dawned on me that Amma wanted me to become free of disease, even more than I did, and She took pains to help me get better. Amma is indefatigable when it comes to freeing anyone, not just me, caught in the grip of illness and suffering.

Over the years, I have seen people suffering from all kinds of diseases finding solace and comfort in Her hands and lap.

Amma draws them close to Her and, with kind words, consoles them. More than anyone else, Her heart aches for them to be free of suffering. How can such a heart be anything other than a Mother's heart?

Years passed. Asthma remained my constant companion, a shackle curbing my freedom. It prevented me from playing with other children, from enjoying a vigorous swim in the back-waters, and even from eating my favorite foods. The slightest change in the environment would result in breathlessness. Medicines gave only temporary relief.

A strange mental state began to envelop me. I could think only about freedom from breathlessness. Modes of treatment changed, as did medicines. Doctors said that because the disease was congenital, I could not get total relief. The sense that I lacked freedom dogged me like a shadow. How ardently I wished to be free from asthma's baleful grip!

All this time, I thought about Amma. I could not forget how much She wanted me to be free of asthma. One day, I told Her that I wanted to be rid of my endless agony. I said that I could think of nothing higher than good health.

Amma hugged me and smiled. She then emphatically said that the disease would be cured. It was not the voice of a sibling I heard. It was the voice of Amma, the Divine Mother, who willed me relief. No one other than Amma can comfort another person like that.

The asthma that had trailed me like a shadow soon left, and has not returned to this day. Amma's sankalpa to relieve me from suffering was fulfilled, and my faith in Her was strengthened. The blessing of faith was yet another gift from Amma.

~

I used to be an ashram resident in its early days. Sugunacchan had donated his house and the 10 *cents* of land (0.1 acres) on which it was situated for the ashram's use. There were limited amenities in the ashram then. All the brahmacharis, including me, stayed together. I aspired to know what lay beyond the known. Every word of Amma would boost our self-confidence and inspire us tremendously. She was also strict about ashram discipline, and did not permit us to violate the daily schedule. Although I never failed to follow the ashram discipline, I was guilty of something else: pride in being Amma's brother.

The person in charge of ashram accommodation and related matters then was Br. Nealu (now Swami Paramatmananda Puri). He was a strict disciplinarian, and would check each of the small huts in which the brahmacharis stayed. One day, I took two mats instead of the one allotted to each person. I thought that if I placed one mat on top of the other, I would not feel so cold. The very moment I lay down, Br. Nealu came into the hut. Seeing the two mats, he said that each person was allowed only one mat. I did not like what he said. Was I not entitled to an extra mat? That was what I thought. I even told him that India was independent, and that the days when a Westerner could order Indians about were long over.

Br. Nealu left the hut. I imagined that he would complain to Amma. I prepared the answers I would give Her. Events unfolded as expected, but the outcome was unexpected. When Amma questioned me, I said that Nealu had no right to implement Amma's rules.

Amma's response was merciless. She said that if I wanted to continue as an ashram resident, I should listen not only to human beings but to a tiny insect even.

Hurt, I walked out of the ashram. I decided to go out and work. I stayed with a friend. As the days passed, my perceptions underwent a drastic change. What had I expected Amma to say? I realized how strong my ego was then.

Feeling very sad, I went back to Amma, prostrated at Her holy feet and confessed my mistake. There was not the least trace of harshness on Her face. Smiling, She drew me close to Her side and explained the need to control the mind. Amma, the physician of the mind, made me understand how silly the ego could be.

~

I spent some days as a priest in the ashram-managed temple at Koorampala, Pandalam. While I was there, I had a painful experience. A local resident tried to destroy the temple. I thought that the temple had to face such a fate owing to lapses in my puja. Pained by the thought, I did not sleep at all that night.

Early the next morning, Swami Amritatmananda Puri came to the temple. He said that Amma had sent him because I was in some trouble. When I heard this, I was not surprised. I realized that one can commune with Amma even from a distance.

I also remember the days when the shadow of the ego fell on me while attending the Vedanta classes, which I thought were harsh. I thought I was ready to renounce all that and move to the Himalayas. Now, I realize that true knowledge of life is not obtained from the *Vedas*, *Puranas* or *Upanishads*, but from the living presence of a Guru like Amma. Every moment in Amma's life conveys an exalted message. Was there any need to wander in search of the Truth when Amma was there right before us as the epitome of spiritual experiences and the Supreme Principle?

∼

In 2004, the coastline of Kerala was lashed by a tsunami. At that time, I was in Alappad, where the ocean waves wreaked the maximum destruction. Seeing many near and dear ones washed away to death shocked and saddened me. I joined the rescue, relief and rehabilitation activities launched under Amma's leadership.

Amma took the bereaved survivors into Her lap and consoled them. At the same time, She also ensured that they would be safe and well looked after. As an eyewitness, I saw how Amma had become the sole refuge of Her children, and was deeply moved.

At that time, I had just learned that I had a heart problem, which doctors said was congenital. In accordance with their advice, I was taking about seven tablets daily. The ravages of the tsunami gave me pause. I thought, "Why consume these medicines when life is so fleeting?"

I decided that if I were destined to be protected by God, that protection would be sufficient. Then and there, I discarded the medicines, which I used to carry with me all the time. I told myself that a mind focused on Amma was good enough, and that there was no need for anything else.

More than a decade has passed since. Now, I do not think about the medicines; my heart condition has not troubled me either. Amma, who had first been a physician of my body, became a physician for my mind. The same faith that redeemed me from the experiences of bodily ills is now removing from my mind the very idea of illness itself. Faith is freeing me from anxieties and internal fears. Through faith, I have gained courage and true awareness. Amma, who embodies the highest truth, has proven to be more than just a physician of the body and mind. She is a doctor of the soul.

(September 2014)

"I taught Amma!"
Selin Rodrigues, India

I would walk from Clappana to the Vallickavu jetty, and then get into a boat. After reaching the far side, I would take a short cut to the Kuzhittura Fisheries School. A sight I once saw on these walks remains clearly imprinted on my mind even today. A girl was sitting cross-legged, immersed in meditation. A thick coil of hair was piled on top of Her head. There was an aura of light around Her face.

As I gazed at Her sitting in solitude on the serene shores of the backwaters, I realized I had taught Her before. She had also been a student of my father, Rodrigues, who had been in charge of the tailoring classes run by the St. Vincent de Paul Society of Clappana Chapel.

~

I got my first job in 1957, teaching at the Cotton Hill School in Trivandrum. When I first wrote 'Selin Rodrigues' and signed my name in the school register, I felt so happy. I taught in that school for three years. After that, I landed a job at the Kuzhittura School. In those days, there was one teacher for each grade in primary school, teaching all the subjects from morning until evening. But by the time I started teaching at the

Kuzhittura School, the school day had become subdivided into periods. My job was to teach English to students of the third and fourth grades.

Hindu philosophy holds that one can attain oneness with God through proximity to a God-realized being. Perhaps, because of some meritorious deed done in some past life, I was blessed to teach English in the third and fourth grades to a girl called Sudhamani, who is known today as Sri Mata Amritanandamayi Devi. She was very smart. I consider having taught Sudhamani the biggest blessing in my life.

In addition to Sudhamani, her sisters Kasturi and Sugunamma and brother Subhagan were also my students.

It was at the end of Her fourth year that Sudhamani developed severe stomach pains. I have taken Her home when she was unable to bear the pain. Sometimes, I would ask Her friends to take Her home. On two occasions, I took Her to the doctor. It was at the dispensary run by the husband of my colleague, Satyavati, that Sudhamani was examined and medicines dispensed.

While Sudhamani was in the fourth grade, I received a few complaints about her from other students:

"In the morning, before coming to school, she goes and sits on the beach;"

"That child sits cross-legged before the roaring waves;"

"The girl is always missing during drill lessons."

Even then, Sudhamani would frequent the beach, gaze at the sea and talk to it. She could commune with nature, but we didn't realize this then. That said, none of the teachers ever had reason to scold Her.

Contrary to what many say, Amma did *not* discontinue Her education after the fourth grade. She passed the fourth grade, and attended fifth-grade classes. I remember seeing Her sitting in the second row of the classroom for fifth graders. Even then, I had taken note of this girl, who was such a brilliant student. But after two or three weeks, Sudhamani stopped coming to school. Later, Her father, Sugunacchan, tried to readmit Her to school, but he had to cross a big bureaucratic hurdle, including obtaining permission from the education authorities in Kollam and Trivandrum. Although Her official education came to an end in the fifth grade, Amma is now Guru to many throughout the world.

My dad was a Father at the Clappana Chapel. When the St. Vincent de Paul Society, associated with the chapel, started tailoring classes, my father was put in charge. Amma, who was studying tailoring in a house in Clappana, started going to the chapel instead to learn tailoring. She studied tailoring with my father for two years.

My father's words come to mind: "Sudhamani was extraordinarily quick on the uptake. You just had to show Her something just once; She would grasp it immediately. She quickly mastered sewing, machine stitching and embroidery."

There were 10 – 15 students in the tailoring class. I remember my father saying that Sudhamani had a distinctive habit: She would go to the cemetery adjoining the chapel and sit by Herself. Her friends also said that they have seen Her sitting near certain tombstones and talking.

It was while She was attending tailoring classes that Amma started Her Bhava darshans. Many people would go to see Amma. I have heard it said that Bhava darshans were held three times a week. However, the Amma who came to my father to study tailoring was an utterly humble student. Although he had grown to admire and respect Sudhamani, my father could not accept the Bhava darshans as he was Christian. Once, my father called Sudhamani and asked Her, "What is Bhava darshan? Why are you doing all this?" I realize that my father wasn't capable of understanding Amma's greatness then. It was in his last days that Amma rose like a star in the spiritual firmament of not just India, but the whole world. The news of how Amma's voice resounded in the halls of the United Nations made headlines in newspapers. My father heard the whole nation singing praises of Her humanitarian projects. He wanted to see Amma, his old student, in person. Twice, he insisted on being taken to Amma, but I was reluctant to take my father, who had become sick and infirm. He then said, "At least, take me to the roadside when Amma is passing Vallickavu."

In the past, whenever I went to see Amma, she would call out, "Hey teacher!" My student, my darling student, has grown into a colossus. Amma, who now lovingly calls me "Daughter," is, for me, Jagadeeshwari, Goddess of the Universe, and Karunamayi, the Compassionate Mother. I have seen Her protect these shores and this land by Her ocean of compassion. I now think it was to live close to this ocean of compassion that I left my job in Trivandrum to come to Kuzhittura.

My father departed from this world on August 3rd, 2008, at the age of 94. We have preserved the shirt he wore on the day he died. In its pocket, we found a photo of Amma. When I saw this, I was astounded, as my father had earlier denied Amma's greatness. I think my father finally discerned who She was. However, I did not fulfill his last wish of seeing Amma.

May Amma forgive me. She will forbear and forgive because Amma is my mother, and She helps everyone. My father's body now rests in the same cemetery that Amma used to visit. I feel sure that his soul is with Amma in a sphere beyond this one. I am ever indebted to Amma for Her love and compassion.

(March 2012)

My Amma
Rajan Maestri, India

I crawled towards Amma, who was sitting in Devi Bhava. She held me close to Her and, pinching both my cheeks, asked, "Son, who brought you here? Who told you that your Mother is here?"

Those compassionate words floored me totally. The image of my mother, whom I had lost when I was 10, came to mind. I was 48 then. What kind of emotions would the memory of a loving mother evoke in the mind of her son? Whatever they may be, it was the maternal love I could not get during my early years that Amma showered on me.

I came to Amma in 1980, when I was in the grip of physical and financial difficulties. I had just given my elder daughter away in marriage. One day, while confiding my problems to a friend, he said, "Rajan Maestri, let's go to a place. All your problems will be solved." Somehow, that trip did not materialize then. A few months later, my friend renewed his invitation. He suggested that we meet at the Kollam bus station the next day at 8:30 p.m. I closed my tailoring shop in Kollam, and got there on time. Even though I insisted on knowing, my friend did not disclose where we were going.

We reached Vallickavu at around 10 p.m. I was fervently praying for a permanent solution to all my problems. My friend said, "Krishna Bhava is over. Amma has started Devi Bhava darshan." His statements did not mean anything to me because Krishna and Devi had never been part of my life. Visiting temples and making offerings had never been my thing, then and now. All I wanted was for my physical and financial difficulties to be mitigated. I could not think of anything else.

~

I started tailoring at the age of 15. My father was a tailor. My son is also a tailor. I am now 78. Every Sunday, I go to Amritapuri, whether or not Amma is physically there. I believe Her presence is always there. After chatting with acquaintances and having lunch, I return home. I have not missed even one Sunday to date.

In those early days, things were very different. Even getting to the ashram was no mean feat. We had to wait for hours along the highway to catch a bus. Bus No. 902 from Kollam bus station would leave at 8:45 p.m. and reach Vallickavu at about 10 p.m. We would take the same bus back at 5:10 a.m. Otherwise, if darshan ended early, we would take a boat from the ashram jetty at 3 a.m. and reach Kollam at 6 a.m.

The ashram did not develop overnight. Amma overcame all opposition with love, and thus moved forward. While walking from Vallickavu junction to the boat jetty, the locals would taunt you if they knew you were new to the area and if they knew you were going to the ashram. I remember one incident. Once in the boat, a youngster slyly remarked, as if talking to himself, "Someone from somewhere comes at midnight and leaves before sunrise." His words were full of innuendo. I didn't like it at all. I boldly moved towards him and sternly asked, "What do you know about Amma?" The young man was taken aback; he hadn't expected this response from me. I continued in the same strain, "When the banana tree bears fruits, when its tiny, flowery bunches open up, bats come at night to sip the honey, and they leave before sunrise. Did you know that?" Everyone in the boat was stunned.

Amma nurtured the ashram not only by standing up to all kinds of opposition but also by giving devotees tough lessons in austerity. She used to give darshan in that tiny 120-square-foot-room in the kalari, with 20 – 25 people crowded around Her. Two devotees would stand on either side to fan Her. Often, Amma would still become drenched in perspiration, and a towel would be used to wipe Her dry. There was no money even to buy a fan. The bhajan singers and visitors would fill the adjoining veranda, which measured about 135 square feet. Amma Herself would distribute the sweets and fruits that devotees brought to everyone. This was usually done after the Krishna Bhava darshan.

A marriage proposal came for my second daughter. I told Amma about it during Devi Bhava. Amma said, "Son, make inquiries, and if you like the proposal, go ahead."

I said, "Amma, I will inquire and report to you by tomorrow."

"There is no darshan tomorrow," Amma said. "Moreover, since Amma is preparing to go abroad, She will have no time."

After making inquiries, I happily returned to the ashram the next day. In those days, there was a hut behind the old prayer hall. I waited there. Hours went by. Some of the ashram residents told me in a friendly tone, "Don't you know that there is no darshan today?"

Hearing this, I became sad and angry. I asked, "Do you expect me to go to America after two days to ask for Amma's decision?" I could not leave. I was worried about how I was going to conduct the marriage. I had about three or four gold sovereigns, but that wasn't enough. I needed at least 25 sovereigns. There were other marriage expenses, too.

Suddenly, I saw someone sitting by my side. I turned and saw Amma. She said in a serious tone, "I am leaving tomorrow. Son, didn't I tell you not to come, and that there would be no darshan today?"

I tried somehow to convey the seriousness of my situation and my helplessness. "Yes, Amma, I know there is no darshan.

But they want the marriage to be performed in two weeks. The groom, who is working in the Gulf, wants to return soon after the wedding. I don't have any money with me!"

Amma took the horoscopes from me and looked at them. She then kissed the horoscopes and returned them, saying, "Son, don't worry about anything. Everything will proceed smoothly."

Hearing this, I felt relieved because if Amma says so, it will happen. I then said, "Someone from the ashram should attend the wedding." Amma shook her head, but I insisted: "That won't do. You must tell someone right now to come."

Amma summoned a brahmachari and said, "There's going to be a marriage in this son's house. Someone from the ashram should attend."

By Amma's grace, everything went off smoothly. Many people — friends and relatives — generously helped with money and gold ornaments. I feel this was Amma showering Her compassion on me. I still wonder how that marriage took place smoothly, without a hitch.

~

I did not have a mother with whom I could be a naughty boy, pestering his mummy. But I made up for it with Amma, who always accepted my mischief.

To make the child in me happy, Amma accepted my invitation to visit my home. After tea and snacks, I said, "Amma, let's go to a movie tonight." She looked at me in wonder. Probably, no one had ever asked Her such a thing. I said, "*Shankarabharanam*[1] is a good movie. Amma must see it for my sake." Amma tried to wriggle out, but I didn't give up. I had sweet dreams of my taking my Mother for a movie, and pouring out my love and affection on Her.

Finally Amma relented. "All right, let it be so. But ask my children first." When the brahmacharis learned that it was *Shankarabharanam*, they also became excited. We arranged a vehicle to go to Kollam. I was like a victor leading his team of 13 or 14. The happiness I felt, however, was commensurate with having conquered all empires. Even now, the waves of that bliss have not left my heart.

Recently, when I went to Her, Amma proclaimed loudly to the people sitting around, "See this old man? He was the one who once took me to a movie!" I looked around. There were many dignitaries present, including a former minister of the central government, a few well-known doctors, and senior officials from Amma's institutions. Devotees from other parts of the world were also there. Why did Amma have to say that

---

1 An award-winning movie glorifying Indian classical music and based on the theme of the Guru-disciple relationship.

about me in front of all those people? Well, that's Amma for you, an innocent mother.

The other day, I told her, "Amma, I am 78 already. If I get my visa, I will leave!"

Amma smiled and said, "No visa now, old man. Go and sit there!"

(August 2010)

First Impressions
Sethuraman Srinivas Kuruvimalai, U.S.A.

I was raised in a remote town in the state of Tamil Nadu, India, in a simple, Hindu family. My mother is a devotee of Devi. I grew up listening to the Devi chants she sang daily. That was my only exposure to spirituality. City life was unknown to me until I moved to Chennai for my bachelor's degree in 1983.

My association with Amma started in 1985. I had just returned home from college when my neighbor, Seshan-acchan, called me and asked me if I could distribute flyers advertising Amma's visit to Chennai. The flyers had Her photo on it. I did not know who Amma was, and asked Seshan-acchan about Her. He told me that Amma was a great saint and that She was visiting Chennai for the first time the week after, and that he would be hosting Her.

I distributed the flyers to about 50 families living in the neighborhood and to some businesses nearby. A week later, Amma arrived in the house next door. I received my first hug in Seshan-acchan's house.

The next day, my dad went for Amma's darshan. After that, he felt a strong urge to invite Her home but was hesitant to ask Her because he did not know Malayalam. Understanding his heart, Amma asked a brahmachari nearby to tell my dad that She would visit our home on the way to the evening program.

When Amma came home that evening at dusk, She walked straight to the puja room and started chanting sacred verses in Malayalam. She sang a couple of bhajans and left after 15 minutes. Before leaving, She gave us some milk as prasad.

I attended that whole week of programs, which took place in various local temples and marriage halls. On one of the evenings, Amma's program was held at the Muruga Ashram. It was a small ashram, but the management wanted Amma to come and sing there. The head priest of the ashram, an ardent devotee of Lord Muruga, performs puja daily to Lord Muruga. When Amma's program was about to commence, he sought Her permission to give a short talk.

He narrated a dream he had had the previous night. Lord Muruga had appeared and told him to dress and decorate the idol as Lord Krishna. He said that Radha, the famed devotee of Krishna, would be coming the next day to sing bhajans. The priest decorated the idol of Muruga as Lord Krishna with a beautiful flute. Seeing the idol, one would not have been able to tell it was Lord Muruga; it looked just like Lord Krishna.

The interesting thing was that this priest had taken a vow to worship only Lord Muruga throughout his life, but at his Lord's behest, he had dressed Him as Krishna. He then requested Amma to sing bhajans.

That evening, Amma sang mostly Lord Krishna's bhajans. A couple of times during the evening, Amma entered the state of *samadhi* (transcendent absorption in the Supreme). There was an absolute stillness around Her. I had not known what samadhi means. A few months before this incident, I had read in *Life of Sri Ramakrishna* about the saint going into samadhi while singing bhajans. Seeing Amma in that super-conscious state thrilled me to no end. The next day, I asked the brahm-acharis (who are now sanyasis) about this state. They told me that it happens all the time with Amma.

Even today, whenever I go to Chennai, I visit the Muruga Ashram and go to the spot where Amma sat. I pray for a few minutes before leaving.

Because this event happened decades ago, I was not sure whether my memory was playing tricks with me. So I called the ashram to check on the facts associated with this incident. The person who answered the call was none other than the priest himself! Now a sanyasi and 93 years old, he still performs puja to Muruga twice daily.

~

The windows of Amma's darshan room in Chennai were always open, and so, from the patio of our house, we could see Amma giving darshan. My brother and I would always sit on the patio, watching Amma give darshan. Many times, She would wave at us and ask us to come over and sit near Her. These patio darshans continued for two years, 1985 and 1986.

We formally invited Amma to our home again in 1986, and She graciously visited our home for the second time. Amma was returning home from a program. Alighting from the van, She asked if it was ok to come home so late. It was 11 p.m. She sat down on the sofa and invited us all to sit with Her. She spoke to us for a long time.

I became emotionally attached to that sofa, so much so that I kept it for almost 10 years after Amma's visit even after it had become worn out. It was only after I went to the U.S. in 1996 that my mum gave the sofa away. I believe that any object a mahatma uses is imbued with spiritual energy.

Amma's third visit to Chennai was in 1987. By this time, the crowd that gathered to have Her darshan had swelled to a few thousand. We had been taking Amma for granted, regarding Her as our next-door neighbor! That year, darshan took place not at our neighbor's but in a palatial bungalow that belonged to a former actress. That was the end of our patio darshans.

I felt left out because I no longer received much attention from Amma. As I stood in the doorway of this house, Amma spotted me and asked me to come and sit near Her. I felt relieved. Over time, I realized that Amma does not outgrow us; rather, She becomes ingrained in us.

~

The Chennai Brahmasthanam Temple was the second such temple that Amma consecrated. Being the political capital of South India, there were many administrative hurdles that needed to be crossed in getting clearance to build an ashram. At a crucial point, a senior government officer, who was also a Shiva devotee, was transferred to Chennai. He became a devotee of Amma and helped us get through the bureaucratic formalities.

At that time, there was a severe drought in Chennai. When volunteers asked Amma about the consecration, She gave a date in May, which fell during a period when the sun's radiation is felt most intensely in South India. When the volunteers told Amma that it would be very hot then, She replied that it would rain heavily that day. True to Amma's words, there was such a downpour in Chennai that day that all the major newspapers attributed it to Amma. When a Master makes a sankalpa, nature obeys.

~

My neighbor, Seshan-acchan, was a great devotee of Amma; so was his wife. He would meditate for three to four hours every day. During one of the Devi Bhava programs, Amma initiated him into a mantra. Within minutes, he went into samadhi, which lasted for about seven hours. He always had inspiring words for me and my wife. Two of his daughters are residents of the Amritapuri ashram, and two granddaughters are brahmacharinis there. Seshan-acchan's example showed me that it is possible for householders to grow spiritually. Memories of seeing him meditate during Amma's first few programs in Chennai inspire me to this day to be regular in my daily meditation.

Although it has been more than 30 years since I first met Amma, I have come to realize that it is not the number of years with Amma that matter. What matters is whether or not we have availed of Her presence to reach or move closer to the goal of human life. Amma's every breath is for the benefit of Her children, and She is ready to take us to the Ultimate if we have the intensity and longing for the goal. I pray that Amma constantly inspires and guides us all in our efforts to attain Self-realization.

(August 2013)

Engaged for Eternity
Rehana Raj T., India

I met my soul mate in 1985. The only unusual thing about this is that millions of other people consider Her their soul mate, too. That soul mate is none other than my Guru and Mother, Sri Mata Amritanandamayi Devi.

My parents took me and my younger brother to Amma when we were very young. When I first saw Amma in a small hut, She was surrounded by a crowd of devotees. Her eyes were sparkling, and She called out to me and my brother. In this way, Amma made us feel special and honored.

During our first darshan, Amma made me and my brother sing bhajans. She called my brother *"paattukaaran mon"* ("singer son"). Today, my brother, Rahul Raj, is a leading music director in the Malayalam film industry. His very first dedication to Amma was *'Lokah samastah sukhino bhavantu,'* the theme song of *Amritavarsham50*, Amma's 50th birthday celebrations.

Meditation camps with Amma were our greatest vacations. I vividly recall the *Hari-kathas*[1] by Swamiji, dances and dramas, spiritual discourses, and delicious afternoon meals. As soon as we crossed the Vallikavu backwaters and reached the ashram, my brother and I would be like uncaged birds. For nine or 10

---

1. Narration of sacred tales, interspersed with singing of bhajans.

days, our parents would leave us alone. What could be more pleasing than that? The ashram, as always, was paradise, sanctified by Amma's presence and permeated by love, bliss and tranquility. Back in the 1980s, Amma was like an easily available goddess! Anybody could gain access to Her anytime. I always felt at home in the ashram.

There was always a large group of children around Amma, who would often play with the children. Her favorite game was 'kallu kali'—throwing stones into the air and catching many with one hand. Whenever we tried, we would drop at least a few stones, but Amma would unfailingly catch them all.

Once, everyone gathered to watch a dance drama called 'Sri Krishna Leela.' Because construction work was going on, there were no proper seating arrangements. The children sat down on the heaps of stones in order to enjoy a good view of the drama. To my surprise, I saw Amma sitting near me. I was so mesmerized by Her magical presence that I forgot to stand up and greet Her. When the play started, Amma tied my frock to the end of Her sari.

After the play's opening act, the beautiful Lord Krishna appeared on stage. Amma stood up and clapped Her hands, and we did the same. As the story started to unfold, we sat down, but Amma continued standing. I tugged Her sari and asked Her to sit down. With utmost gravity, Amma replied, "How can I sit down when my Krishna is standing up?" I realized that for Amma, She was not seeing just a play; She beholds God everywhere and in everything.

When the play ended, Amma immediately left for Her room, dragging me because of the knot She had tied. Noticing it, She gave me a big smile and untied the knot. I wholeheartedly wished that She had not done that; I wanted to be with Her always. I had the privilege of associating closely with Her for seven years. Although the knot was untied, I feel that I am still with Her. A disciple's divine romance with the Guru never ends.

~

My mother used to frighten me by saying that God watches everything from heaven. This was her way of ensuring that I would not throw my milk out of the window, or pinch my brother. My simple faith that Amma was God, and therefore omnipresent, made me wonder if She knew all my secrets.

I had read in Amma's biography about the miraculous experience of a girl whom Amma had appeared before during her examinations (visible only to her) to help her answer the questions. Fascinated by the story, I yearned to have the same experience. When my exams drew near, I did 'special' *Lalita Sahasranama* archanas, without studying! During my final exams, I waited for Amma to appear in the exam hall. I was so sure that She would walk through the door that I kept staring at the door. This caught the attention of the invigilator. For half an hour, I did not write anything on the answer sheet. Then my hopes started dying. I felt angry with Amma. Somehow, I finished writing my answers in the rest of the available time.

The week after my exams, I went to the ashram. By then, I had forgotten all about the incident. During darshan, Amma asked, "Darling daughter, did you get frightened in the examination hall? Did you cry thinking of me?"

After recovering from my shock, I asked Amma, "Why didn't You help me in my exams, like you did the other girl?"

Amma laughed and asked, "Did you study sincerely?"

"No."

With utmost sweetness, Amma said, "If you had studied well but had forgotten what you learned, as that girl had, then I would have definitely helped you. Nevertheless, Amma heard your prayers. If we try sincerely and then leave the results to God, He will answer our prayers."

Amma's answers convinced me. Even though She had not physically appeared before me in the examination hall, She had clearly demonstrated that She was all-knowing. I can never hide anything from Her!

~

In my family, all of us except my dad used to have beautiful Amma dreams. Rahul and I would boast about our dreams as soon as we woke up. If I carefully studied my dreams of Amma, I would find the meaning very clear.

As a student, I was lazy, and my dad would bring a bamboo cane home (just to scare me). I used to throw it into the plot of land next to our house. One day, when my exams were nearing, I dreamt of Amma in Devi Bhava. She was wearing a beautiful green sari and holding a bamboo cane in Her hands! Amma started to scold me for not studying. She asked, "Will you throw the cane over the wall again?" Terrified, I started running away. Amma ran after me! At last, I surrendered to Her and promised that I would not throw the cane away again.

Frightening though the dream was, I did not take it seriously. During my next darshan, Amma asked me, "Darling daughter, do I have to carry a stick and make you run around before you become obedient?"

My dad was a little disappointed at not having Amma dreams. But one day, he had a beautiful dream. Amma came near his bed and sat down near his head. She caressed his hair, touched his forehead and slowly whispered, "Dear son, don't be sad." He did not tell us about this dream. That weekend, unable to control his yearning to see Amma, he visited the ashram all alone. When Amma saw him, She exclaimed, "You rogue! You saw me in your dreams, didn't you!" Tongue-tied, my father shed a few drops of tears on Amma's feet.

My dad was a chronic asthma patient, who, at one time, was more often in the hospital than at home. He tried all kinds of treatment, but nothing worked. Hindus believe that all suffering is the karma created by bad actions done in the past. My father told Amma that he wanted to experience his prarabdha minimally. She assured him that She would take his asthma away. His hospital visits became less and less frequent.

Once, my dad suffered from a particularly severe asthma attack and stopped breathing. He was rushed to the hospital, where the doctors gave him defibrillator shocks, to no avail. My brother and I were in school then. Shocked and feeling utterly helpless, my mother called out to Amma. She chanted her mantra continuously and then started chanting the *Lalita Sahasranama*. By Amma's grace, my dad started to breathe again.

That evening, someone from the ashram came home, bearing prasad from Amma, holy ash and a beautiful letter in Amma's own handwriting. The person narrated how restless Amma had been that day, and had told him that "something has happened to my *vakeel mon* (lawyer son). Go now and meet him!" This is what Amma had written:

Dear son,

Don't be sad, my little child. I was worried about you. Pray to Almighty God. Amma will also pray for you. Amma is with you. Don't think you are alone and helpless. Amma is there for you. Make your mind strong. Amma's kisses for you!

Later, Amma told my mother, "How strong your call was that day! I couldn't resist thinking of you."

~

Amma consecrated the Brahmasthanam Temple at Chennai in May 1990. At that time, Chennai had been facing a severe drought for a long time, but Amma had assured devotees that it would rain on the day of the consecration. Her words had spread like wildfire. Eager to see the prophecy fulfilled, we followed Amma to Chennai. Accommodation was in a nearby school. We forgot all discomforts in the awareness that Amma was just a few doors away. All my thoughts were saturated with remembrances of Amma.

On May 6th, as Amma was performing the *kalasha puja* on top of the temple, we saw eagles flying around in the skies right above the temple. (This auspicious sign has been observed in all the consecration ceremonies of Amma's Brahmasthanam temples.) And then, it started raining. There was loud applause and big smiles all around. No one ran away, preferring to be soaked by the downpour. The next day, even newspaper headlines proclaimed Amma's shower of blessings.

There was water everywhere! The tent, where devotees were seated, became flooded with water. And yet, everyone remained focused on the pujas. Rain drops were eager to touch Amma, too. Her beautiful face was adorned with crystalline drops of rain, which She did not wipe away. Divine love mesmerized the crowd, suspending our body consciousness.

I was seated in the last row, keenly observing Amma. I thought that it was unlikely that Amma would even notice me in that huge crowd. I was so 'love-struck' by Amma's grace and power that I was not aware of how drenched I was from head to toe. I entered a meditative trance and thought, "How ravishing is Her beauty, just like Sri Krishna! I wish I could look like Her! May my every cell be transformed so that I become Amma!"

Volunteers were standing with towels to wipe devotees' heads and faces before they went for darshan. After queuing up in the long darshan line, I finally reached Amma. When a volunteer tried to wipe my head, Amma stopped her and said, "No! Just let her be." She gave me a tight hug, kissed my cheeks and forehead, and pinched my chin. I stood still, like a doll. Hot tears were rolling down my cheeks. Lifting my chin, Amma said, "I saw you looking at me when you were sitting in the last row. Tell me, what you were thinking? I know what it was, but I want to hear it from you!" I was too shy to speak. Amma gave another tight hug and whispered in my ears, "My daughter, you look just like me!"

~

Years ago, many people gathered in the Kali Temple to listen to a talk by a famous orator. As he spoke, there was pin-drop silence. My eyes wandered around in search of Amma, and found Her sitting at the back on the bare floor, with no one near Her. Gathering all my courage, I went and sat just a foot away from Her, face to face. Amma did not say anything. She just looked at me and smiled, as if I were some harmless creature. To my surprise, Amma took my hands in Hers. She opened my palms and started looking at them. She then began to press some of the lines. I felt that Amma was reading my future and 'correcting' my fate line. I simply let Her do whatever She was doing. After some time, Amma started to peel off my nail polish with Her nails. When She saw the red-stoned ring on my ring finger, She removed it from my finger and tried to wear it on Her little finger. The blockhead that I was, I begged Her to return my ring; I said that my mum would scold me if I lost it. Amma just smiled, like Sri Krishna, and continued holding on to it for some more time. When the satsang was about to end, Amma hurriedly got up, put the ring back on my finger, and pinched my index finger lovingly. Her face expressed utmost compassion.

I still recall that short, silent and secret encounter with Amma with wonder. The 'pinch mark' grew with my growing skin, and it reminds me to this day of my blissful engagement with eternity.

(September 2014)

"Amma is still the same!"
Priyan (Fouad Nassif), Lebanon

Vyasa (Gregory McFarland, U.S.A.) has been a devotee of Amma for more than 30 years. Recently, he visited Amritapuri for a month to be with Amma for Her 60th birthday celebrations. Even though he has been meeting Amma every year in the U.S. since Her first World Tour in 1987, it has been 18 years since he last visited Amritapuri. He shared his memories of his earliest visits to Amritapuri in 1982 and 1983.

"In 1979, when I was living in Santa Fe, New Mexico, a friend who knew of my interest in Buddhism and Zen Buddhism told me about a young spiritual seeker who followed the Hindu tradition and was living in India. He was visiting his family in Santa Fe for a short time. This is how I met Br. Nealu (now Swami Paramatmananda Puri). He hadn't met Amma yet but had been doing very strict sadhana in Tiruvannamalai and serving Swami Ratnamji, who had been a personal attendant to Ramana Maharshi Himself. Nealu's knowledge of the Hindu scriptures was impressive, and he obviously was a serious sadhak, following a strict regimen of spiritual practices, despite his frail health. I enjoyed interacting with him. He returned to India shortly afterwards.

"About three years later, I met Nealu's cousin at a grocery store, and he told me that Nealu was back for a visit. I was interested in meeting him again. When I did, I was moved by his warmth and loving nature. He shared with me his most recent experiences. With great enthusiasm and liveliness, Nealu told me that he had met a great Indian young woman in Kerala who was a mahatma, that She had become his Guru, and that he now lived in Her ashram. He showed me photos of Amma and played an audio cassette of Her singing. As I began discovering bits and bytes about Amma, I began to feel more and more convinced that I had to go to India at the earliest to meet Her — and maybe stay there for good!

"Nealu was travelling back in three weeks. It didn't seem possible and reasonable for me to accompany him. I was living with my wife and young son, and had a job and responsibili-ties. I needed a passport and visa, and had to deal with some property issues. Still, like magic, everything was resolved in time, and without any hitch, I was able to join Nealu on his next trip to India to see Amma in August 1982.

"Our plane landed in Madras, and I remember being com-pletely exhausted by the travel. Nealu was so sick and weak that I wondered if he would make it to Kerala! He had brought with him many boxes of things. This held us up at the airport customs for hours. Finally, we were 'released,' and we immedi-ately found a hotel to rest for a couple of days before flying to Trivandrum. From there, we took a taxi to Vallickavu. The heat, humidity and discomforts of the ride wore me down completely.

I remember Amma coming to meet us outside and giving me a first hugging darshan.

"The ashram then consisted of a cowshed next to the house that belonged to Amma's parents. Amma used to give darshan and hold the Krishna and Devi Bhava darshans in this cowshed. A short distance from the cowshed, there were two rows of thatched huts in an L-shaped formation. They were partitioned into about 12 smaller huts. I stayed with Nealu in one of these huts. Amma had a hut, where She met people during the day. At night, She slept in a room inside Her parents' house. The other huts were occupied by other disciples or seekers who stayed with Amma. All around were coconut groves, swamps, backwaters and open areas where we would wash or help with household activities. The ashram had not been officially established, and Amma's father had just allowed a few brahmacharis to stay in the huts next to the house. The first brahmacharis were Unni (Swami Tureeyamritananda), Balu (Swami Amritaswarupananda), Venu (Swami Pranavamritananda, who became a best friend), Sri Kumar (Swami Purnamritananda), Ramakrishna (Swami Ramakrishnananda, who hadn't yet left his job at a bank), Rao (Swami Amritatmananda) and, of course, Nealu.

"Before I could really settle in with Nealu in his hut and rest, I was told that a big event was to start shortly. It was Krishna Bhava! Crowds started flocking to the place.

"My first experience of the Bhava darshans was totally mysterious. It was way too much for me to comprehend. Mars might have been easier to understand! And as soon as the beaming Krishna left, Devi replaced Him with Her crown and special garments! Nothing in my life so far had prepared for me for such an experience. Nealu had spoken to me about the Bhava darshans, but the first-hand experience was way more than what the mind and intellect could process.

"During those days, I remember that we often discussed among ourselves whether Amma was just channelling Krishna and Devi during the Bhava darshans, mimicking them, being possessed by them, or simply fully being them. I concluded after my first encounter that Amma was none other than Devi, the Goddess Herself, and none other than the historical Krishna Himself. Nealu had studied the scriptures and used them to prove that this was the case, and his arguments were very convincing. I remember asking Her once, still intrigued by the Bhava darshans, 'Is Devi real?'

"She answered with a smile, 'She is as real as you are!'

"About 300 to 600 devotees would come for the Bhava darshans, which took place three days a week, giving me barely enough time to rest from these repeated, all-night, sleepless events!

"Amma was literally with us all the time. She ate with us (we had our meals in Sugunacchan's house), fed us, meditated with us, and sang bhajans with us. Bhajans took place right outside the cowshed.

"I fell sick once, and Amma would come to check on me regularly, showing care and concern. At the same time, She made me feel that the sickness of the body was not that important!

"The goal for all of us back then was Self-realization. Everyone did intense practices to get closer to this goal. I asked Amma once, 'When will I know that I have become realized?'

"She answered, 'When you realize that you are none other than me!'

"On another occasion, I asked Her about the *Hatha Yoga* practices that I was trying to maintain daily. She didn't give it any importance, giving me the impression that She felt my doing these exercises might encourage my ego and pride. As soon as I realized this, Amma said that it was okay if I continued doing my yoga. But now I had become aware that I should not become identified with it. Once, She also warned me not to start *pranayama* practices without the guidance of a Realized Master."

When asked if he had ever imagined that the ashram would become what it is today, Vyasa answered, "Absolutely not! The focus then was just on doing spiritual practices, mainly meditation and devotional singing, and spending maximum time with Amma, with the goal of attaining God-realization. Even seva was considered an excuse for the ego to disrupt the practices.

But Amma felt the need to make us feel more compassion for others. By serving them, we became less self-centered. Everything happened at the right time, as She must have planned it. But I never thought that Her mission would include numerous charitable works, institutions, etc. I never ever dreamt that there would be high-rise buildings in the ashram!

"But from 1987 onwards, when She started Her World Tours, I realized that She would make Her presence felt in the world, and that Her mission would become global. Still, all this is a miracle, as in 1982 – '83, the few who lived with Her had barely enough.

Once, seeing the pitiful conditions of the kitchen utensils, plates, cups and spoons, I went to Oachira with a couple of 'hut boys' (as the brahmacharis were called), and purchased a whole set of new stainless steel plates, cups, spoons and cooking vessels. It was on that day that we met an *avadhuta*[1] named Prabhakara Siddha Yogi. Watching the way he behaved was a mind-blowing experience for me. Later, he visited Amma, and I remember how much Amma enjoyed watching him be his totally free self.

"But what I remember most from that trip to Oachira was that on our way back, one of the brahmacharis informed me that the night before, Amma had told him that it would be

1 An enlightened person whose behavior transcends social norms.

good to get some new kitchen utensils. I was stunned! I felt that Amma's mere sankalpa was so powerful that the universe would move to fulfill it! I was happy to have been a humble instrument. I realized She was more in control of my mind than I, and was shaken by this thought.

"Initially, I intended to stay for at least three years. But I found that I was still attached to various things in the world, and didn't want to deny this. I was particularly missing my young boy, whom I had left behind in Santa Fe. So I stayed for three months, from August to October 1982, and then flew back home.

"But my daily connection to Amma remained very strong. I had photos of Her, bhajan cassettes, and a video, which I started showing around while sharing my experience. One person who was immediately and irresistibly touched by Amma was a young woman living in my neighborhood. She came to India with me when I returned a few months later in 1983 with my teenage daughter. That young woman was Kusuma, who helped organize Amma's first visit to the U.S. in 1987.

"When I returned, I saw a few more huts and a few more people living with Amma. The ashram had been legally registered with the government. Also, the cowshed had been dismantled and was now replaced by a more solid cement structure, the kalari.

"Today, it is the only place that remains as it was back then. It was where I received my *mantra diksha* (initiation) from Amma on October 2nd, 1982. Rao also received initiation on the same day. I remember the date because after my initiation, I went to my hut and Nealu took a photo of me with a calendar showing the date hanging right behind me. That morning, I had asked Amma for a mantra. She had agreed and had said that She would do it after the Krishna and Devi Bhavas. She instructed me to take a shower before the start of the Bhava darshans. According to the tradition, I took a shower with my clothes on. She asked me to prepare a plate of fruits and then wait behind the cowshed until the very end, when She would send someone to call me. I was in a very elevated state. Amma received me in the cowshed. There was only one other person with us, a brahmachari. She made me sit on Her *peetham* (sacred chair) and whispered the mantra in my right ear while the brahmachari closed my left ear."

I asked him about the photos that he had taken inside the kalari. These are the oldest surviving photos of Amma's Krishna and Devi Bhavas. Vyasa responded, "They are truly unique and very precious. Nealu felt that it was not appropriate for him to take photos. So he pushed me to carry the camera, go inside the temple during the Bhava darshans, and take photos. I did. No one was pleased with this, but Amma didn't seem bothered by it. I started clicking and clicking, each time daring to get closer to Amma and trying various angles. Sometimes I was just two feet away from Her!

"Some of the most special photos I took are those of Amma giving darshan to Dattan, the leper, and licking his wounds. I remember that in 1983, I was once in Oachira and heard someone calling me. I turned back and it took me a moment to realize that it was Dattan. His wounds had been fully healed, the skin was dry, and parts of his face had regenerated.

"Because everyone was uncomfortable with me taking the photos, I once took the opportunity to ask Amma whether it was a problem and if I should stop. Her answer was striking: 'In this, do whatever you feel, but don't hesitate!'

"Another time, as we were casually gathered around Her, some brahmacharis expressed how difficult it was to pronounce my name (Gregory). Amma said, 'Then from now on, he will be Vyasa!' That's how I got my name!"

Vyasa is also known for something else. For many years, he has been making *kai-manis* (hand cymbals) for the ashram and for Amma. He explained how this started.

"During my first visits here, when listening to the bhajans, I felt that everything was perfectly in tune except for the kai-manis, which seemed out of tune. I took a pair with me to the U.S. and tried to fix it. It was very refined work. So, I began to study bell metals and bell physics, and decided to try and make new kai-manis myself. After further research, I found the correct metal blend needed and the best proportions to use, and I taught myself how to make models and started casting them (putting the metal into molds). I then worked on fine tuning them to get the ideal sounds. From then on, each year when Amma visited the U.S., I would have improved sets of kai-manis to give the swamis. Amma also has a pair that I made for Her. She carries it around the world with Her. Every time She uses it, She reminds those around about Vyasa, the old-time American devotee who learned how to make them. She often adds that I was one of the first Americans to travel all the way from the U.S. to meet Her in India!

"Right now, while I am at Amritapuri, I am teaching the musicians here how to improve the sound and quality of the kai-manis that they use, and eventually how to make them."

When asked what he feels about Amma's 60th birthday celebrations, Vyasa says, "I think all this doesn't mean anything to Her. She is happy just because people use this occasion to be happy themselves. I see clearly that the real Amma is still the same. One can still receive the exact same spiritual benefit from coming to Her, provided one opens up properly. She still gives very generously. She did it before to fewer people and now to millions. But She is still the same person, unaffected by the numbers or by any other consideration.

"She still finds the best ways to reach the deeper layers in each one and make him or her growth spiritually. She is unique.

She was so in 1982, when I first met Her and when She was just 29 years old, and still is today as She turns 60!"

(September 2013)

The Crossing

My Mother
Br. Eknath, India

There are people who do good deeds, even though they do not believe in God. They help the poor and needy. I have seen how Amma makes such people sit near Her when they go for darshan. Perhaps, it is a blessing for their good deeds.

I know one such man. He was the late B.K. Tripathi. I met him when I went to the Kumbhamela[1] in Allahabad in 2001 to help set up a stall for the ashram. He accommodated me in his house during the time it took to set up the stall. Even though Mr. Tripathi had retired as the Chief Engineer of the Irrigation Department in Uttar Pradesh, his house was simple and unostentatious. In the living room, there was a big, framed photograph of an old woman. She was holding a stick in one hand; the other hand was resting on her knee. She looked like a beggar. Beneath the photo was a caption. As the text was in Bhojpuri,[2] I did not know what it said. My curiosity aroused, I asked him who she was. My mother, he said. Mr. Tripathi then narrated the following story.

~

1 Religious festival that takes place once every 12 years.

2 North Indian dialect.

"I graduated as the top student from the Engineering school of IIT, Kharagpur.[3] I found a job in the Irrigation Department of the Uttar Pradesh government. In due course, I became Chief Engineer, receiving an attractive salary and other perks. One of my assignments was the construction of a dam. Interference from certain lobbies halted this project temporarily. However, those of us in the project team continued receiving our monthly salaries, even though we had no work. During the enforced break, my colleagues and I would spend our time playing cards and partying.

"One day, an old woman came into our office. She must have been in her 80s, at least. She asked me, 'My son, when will the work on the dam resume? My stomach is burning with hunger. Please give some work to these old hands.' Instead of sympathizing with her, we taunted and humiliated her. We imagined that our rough treatment would deter her from coming to the office again.

"We were wrong. She continued coming every day, pleading with us to give her some work. 'My dear child, when will the work on the dam resume? I am very hungry. Please give these old hands some work!' It was the same old lament. The hardhearted man that I was, I continued taunting her mercilessly.

---

3 One of India's best universities.

I was so cross that I even imitated the way she walked and talked!

"One day, my cruelty reached its peak. I brought a camera to work. When the old lady came and started pleading as usual, I took out the camera and took a photo of her. This struck my colleagues and me as hilarious. My tendency then was to derive pleasure from someone else's pain.

"Later that day, my colleagues and I went hunting in a nearby forest. I rode atop an elephant. At one point, I saw a fawn. Taking aim, I released an arrow that hit the fawn on its flank. With a whimper, the baby deer collapsed. It turned its head to gaze at me, its eyes reflecting profound pain, hurt and sorrow. In a few moments, it died. I did not feel any sympathy.

"That evening, when I returned home, I learnt that my young son was having a fever. My wife took him to the doctor, who injected him on the side of his hips. The injection had an adverse effect: my son's leg became paralyzed for life! To say that this incident shocked me would be an understatement. In my mind, my son's plight seemed connected somehow to what I had inflicted on the deer that afternoon. Fate had dealt my son a cruel blow on the exact spot where I had shot the fawn. It seemed like too much of a coincidence. Had God dispensed the fruits of my earlier karma in this way?

"That night, when I went to bed, I started thinking about what I had done that day: the fawn, my son, the old woman, her pleas, my merciless response... I was young, educated and earning a handsome salary, even though all I did was waste my time and money in idle and selfish pursuits. That woman, on the other hand, was an aged destitute. Even so, she did not beg. She wanted some work, so that she could make an honest living. She had dignity and a noble *samskara* (culture), which I lacked despite my so-called education. Her spirit of self-reliance, even at that age and in spite of the abuses she faced daily, was amazing. The least I could do was respect her integrity, not insult her. She could have been my mother or grandmother. What a brute I was! For the first time, the memory of her bent body and cracked voice brought tears to my eyes. I started hating myself. In anguish, I started crying. My weeping continued for the whole night.

"When I got up the next morning, I was a changed person. I went to the photo studio, got the photo developed and framed. I wrote the words uttered by that old woman, beneath the photo. I also prepared some food personally with the intention of feeding her, begging forgiveness, and seeking her blessings. When I went to the office, I waited for that old woman to come. But she never came. Over the next few days, I started searching for her. Despite my best efforts, I could not find her. I think that she had come only to awaken my conscience. I labeled the photo 'My Mother.'

"From that day onwards, I would start each day's work only after gazing at that photo. It kept alive the thought of the poor and needy. The memory of the woman's integrity also put a stop to my corrupt practices, which led to conflicts with my colleagues. But I was determined to abide by my principles. I would set aside money for my expenses and distribute whatever remained to the poor and needy. I would even borrow money to help them. Though I never prayed, I felt sure that there was a divine power supporting me.

"When I retired, I did not receive any gratuity. With whatever money I had, I tried to repay all my debts. Even after all my money had run out, I still owed ₹120,000. During this time, my daughter's marriage was fixed, but I had no money to conduct the marriage. Nobody would have believed this, as I had been Chief Engineer when I retired. I feared that my prospective son-in-law would back out of the marriage if he learnt about my financial situation. Nevertheless, I had strong faith that the good deeds I had done would insure me against misfortune. Also, my conscience told me that I had not hurt anyone after that fateful day. The marriage drew closer. Even four days before the wedding, no arrangements had been made.

"At that point, I received a phone call from Kanpur. It was the bridegroom's mother. She said, 'We have only one son, and he has requested us to ensure that the wedding ceremony be kept simple. He specifically said that his father-in-law should not spend a lot of money on the marriage, as that was his Guru's wish. As we are all going to the U.S. after his marriage, and as we have a lot of property in Kanpur, we are sending you two truckloads of items needed for the marriage. All you have to do is get the two trucks unloaded at your end.'

"I was dumbfounded. Divine providence had not failed me! The marriage was a grand success. I did not have to spend a single rupee. Among the gifts my son-in-law gave me were a biography of Amma, and a subscription to *Matruvani*. Until then, I had never thought about God or revered any deity. After reading Amma's biography, I felt so much veneration for Her that I shed tears. From *Matruvani*, I came to know that Amma is guiding many people along the right path. Along with the experiences I read in *Matruvani*, I learnt about Amma's teachings first hand through my son-in-law, who practices Her teachings. It was Amma's advice that had made him see to it that I did not have to spend money on the marriage. My daughter also told me how her husband had become a changed person after meeting Amma and having Her darshan.

"I began pining for Amma's darshan. My family and I finally got a chance to see Her during Her New Delhi program. When my turn for darshan came, Amma bent over, resting one hand on Her knee, upturning the other. I was stunned! At that moment, She reminded me so much of that old woman, my

Mother! In my heart of hearts, I felt that she had been none other than Amma."

~

The first darshan itself had a tremendous impact on Mr. Tripathi. Thereafter, he dedicated his time to promoting *Matruvani*. He drew up a list of 50 well-known people in Allahabad, and sent them each a copy of *Matruvani*, at his own cost. He also indicated that if they liked *Matruvani* and wanted to subscribe, they should send ₹40 (the annual subscription fee in India then). The response to this marketing campaign was wonderful. One person even sent Mr. Tripathi ₹2,000 to support his *Matruvani* campaign! In his letter to Mr. Tripathi, he explained that Amma had appeared in his dreams, but he had no idea who the woman in white was. But when he received the copy of *Matruvani* that Mr. Tripathi sent, he realized, to his joy, that She was Amma, revered by millions as a mahatma. He also lauded Mr. Tripathi for his service, and encouraged him to continue with his good work.

With the ₹2,000, Mr. Tripathi began sending the magazine to many other people. Some of those who got *Matruvani* wrote back, expressing interest in buying other ashram publications as well. Mr. Tripathi's dedication to his *Matruvani* campaign intensified. To fill up the receipt books, he enlisted the help of students and teachers. Within six months, he collected a thousand subscriptions. He also helped us a lot during the 2001 Kumbhamela.

In March 2001, during the Delhi Brahmasthanam festival, Amma blessed the marriage of Mr. Tripathi's son, whose leg had been paralyzed. She also initiated the couple into a mantra. It was about four in the morning. Mr. Tripathi approached me later and said, "Amma has really blessed me. I used to worry a lot about my handicapped son. Now, by blessing his marriage, I feel that She has taken him into Her lap. Another thing: is there any Guru in this world who is so gracious as to initiate devotees during the *brahma muhurta*?"[4]

In June 2001, he went to a friend's house. He brought with him all the *Matruvani* receipt books and the cash he had collected for the subscriptions. These, he handed over to his friend, saying, "Please continue with this work. I think my time has come. I have a feeling that I will be passing on soon." The friend chided Mr. Tripathi for being morbid. But Mr. Tripathi's request prevailed. The next morning, he passed away. He was 71.

~

---

4 A period of 96 minutes from before sunrise, considered auspicious for spiritual activities.

In September that year, a judge from the Allahabad Court went to Amritapuri to participate in Amma's Birthday. He reached a day too late. The Birthday celebrations had ended. As Amma had been giving darshan for the last three days, many felt that She was not likely to come out of Her room. But to everyone's surprise, Amma came for the evening bhajans that day. After bhajans, She invited the judge to Her room. He spent almost three hours with Her. During their talk, Amma asked him how he had heard about Her. He told Amma that Mr. Tripathi had sent him a copy of *Matruvani*, which had inspired him to meet Amma.

At the mention of his name, Amma's eyes filled with tears. She said, "Amma can clearly see the face of Her son, Tripathi. Until his last breath, he was thinking only about Amma and how he could help propagate Her mission. By thinking about Amma all the time, he had become one with Amma. He passed away in that state, thus attaining Liberation." Amma continued talking for a long time about Mr. Tripathi.

Mr. Tripathi had only had Amma's darshan four or five times. But he had found a special place in Amma's heart because of his selflessness and his service to the poor and needy — all of it dedicated to his Mother.

(December 2004)

Visitation from Amma

Madhuree Biswas, India

Ma had been sick for the last few months. She was staying with my brothers in our hometown in Jeypore. Twice a day, I would talk to her over the phone. Gradually, she became very weak, something I could sense over the phone. But it did not occur to me that her health would deteriorate so rapidly. She was only 69 years old, and still quite active. Whenever she experienced a respite from her sickness, she would become enthusiastic. My mother was an optimistic, kind-hearted and broad-minded woman. Although she was illiterate, her thinking was very modern.

On June 22nd, 2009, I was in my head office in Gurgaon when I received a call at 2:00 p.m. from my *Dada* ('eldest brother,' in Bengali) He said that Ma's condition was deteriorating. I became worried. At 8:00 p.m., Dada called again to tell me that Ma was slipping into a coma. I told Dada to take Ma immediately to Vishakhapatnam, the nearest city, where she could receive advanced medical treatment. My hometown did not have even basic diagnostic facilities like ECG or sonography equipment.

I could not sleep that whole night. Every 30 minutes, I would call Dada to inquire about Ma's condition. Every minute, I was pleading with Amma to let me see my Ma alive just one more time.

~

I had taken Ma to meet Amma in Delhi during Amma's 2006 North India tour. During darshan, when Amma said something in her ear, Ma thought Amma had given her a mantra. She happily told everyone she knew that Amma had blessed her with a mantra. Someone told her that Amma had probably said "My dear child" in Oriya or Malayalam, but I knew Ma was not convinced. She was always wondering what that mantra was. Sometimes, she would even ask me if I knew what it was. After that darshan, she added a photo of Amma to the pictures of gods and goddesses she had in her puja room. She wanted to visit Amritapuri, but her health was too delicate to permit her to undertake such a long journey. Whenever I visit Amritapuri, I would miss her very much and pray for her good health. To this day, I regret not having taken her to Amritapuri.

~

Dada, his wife, my younger brother and his wife reached Vishakhapatnam with Ma the next day. At 2:30 p.m., Ma was admitted into Seven Hills Hospital, one of the best hospitals there. By Amma's grace, I managed to get a flight ticket a few hours later, and reached Vishakhapatnam at 4:30 p.m. I rushed to the hospital without even collecting my luggage at the airport. I was trying to be courageous enough to face the worst. At the same time, I was praying fervently to Amma to heal my Ma. By the time I reached her, Ma was already in a coma. She was hooked to a ventilator, and was struggling to breathe, as guttural sounds issued from deep within her. I was overcome by fear but put on a brave front, as I could see that everyone, even Dada, was frightened, confused and sad. I reminded myself that Amma was with us, and that She would take care of everything.

I put sacred ash from Amma on Ma's forehead and chest. I wanted to put a little in her mouth but the doctors did not allow me to do so. By the next day, her situation had deteriorated further. There was no sign or symptom of life except for the mechanical pumping of air by the ventilator. Dada and I realized how critical Ma's condition was, and we were prepared for the worst. My younger brother, however, was inconsolable. I could sense how much he feared losing my mother. Among Ma's four children, he was the youngest. He had never seen our father, as my father had died as a result of a cerebral-vascular stroke while Ma was pregnant with my youngest brother. He was very attached to Ma. At times, when the reality of Ma's imminent death hit home, he would rush out of the hospital to go to the seashore or to a temple. At one point, he came and told me that one of his friends had suggested a life-saving homeopathic medicine. I asked the doctor if we could give it to Ma, and he agreed.

Suddenly, I thought, "Why not add some of Amma's sacred ash to the medicine?" I did just that.

We were counting the hours, anticipating the worst. I spent the night dozing in the hospital lounge. Early in the morning, before entering the Critical Care Unit, I asked the doctor on night duty about Ma. He said that she had opened her eyes half an hour ago. When I went to her, I called her and she responded to my call! It was difficult for me to contain my joy and my gratitude to Amma. The doctors were surprised and happy at the progress Ma was showing. They said that if she sustained this response and if there was no further infection, she might recover, even though one or some of her organs might become impaired.

Ma's condition continued improving for the next two or three days. Then, all of a sudden, her health started deteriorating again. A fungal infection that started with her eyes gradually invaded her vital organs. This time, the decline was sharper. Dada became distraught. Somehow, by Amma's grace, I was able to ease the distress of my siblings, although it was painful for me to witness her slow and increasingly painful dying and the failure of her vital organs. I watched how helpless a human body can be. The beautiful body, which we cherish so much, which our near and dear ones love so much, is just a bundle of flesh and blood functioning with the help of a few vital organs that can malfunction and fail. When impaired, the body with which we enjoyed worldly pleasures can cause us excruciating pain. I mentally surrendered Ma's fate to Amma.

I did not know if Ma was feeling pain in her body. There was no expression on her face; it was as if she was in deep sleep, unaware of all the ills assaulting her body. But after some time, I could no longer endure the sight of her dying. I earnestly prayed to Amma to release her from all pain.

On July 4th, at about 3:00 p.m., when I was sitting near Ma, I suddenly saw Amma standing near us! I don't know how She appeared there. It wasn't a dream. Her unique rose-sandal fragrance was unmistakably present. She was so close to me that I could have touched Her with my fingers. Before I could do anything, Amma blew once on my Ma's face, into her eyes. The next moment, Amma was not there. I thought, "Ma will be alright, for Amma has blessed her." A few seconds later, doctors and nurses rushed in, saying that Ma was in a critical condition. They administered injections, chest thrusts, etc. At 3:40 p.m., doctors declared Ma dead.

While doctors were trying to revive her, I sensed that Ma had already been released from her body by the power of Amma's breath. She had relieved my mother of all pain. How blessed

Ma was. The experience of Amma's grace at the moment of Ma's death helped me realize yet again the great blessing we have in having Amma with us on earth.

(March 2010)

Boundless Compassion

Bri. Niranjanamrita Chaitanya, India

Many of us move around with unfounded fears, including that of death. There are many who, approaching the threshold of old age, morbidly wonder, "Am I going to die soon?" Could there be anyone who would welcome death, like a householder eagerly receiving a guest? Yes, I have seen one such man: my father. When I reflect that his were the hands I held while toddling, and that I had trailed his shadow to the presence of Amma, I feel immensely gratified.

When he died, he wanted his body given to medical students. To this end, my father prepared all the necessary official documents, which he kept in a cloth bag. I am writing about him, not out of a daughter's attachment to her father or from pride. When one plants a sapling — whether a plantain, mango, coconut or *tulasi* (basil) sapling — one hopes that it will offer shade and support to others; this thought is the essence of spirituality. It is also a form of sharing. Even if it is a *laddu* (Indian sweet), we know how much more enjoyable it is when we share it with two or three other people.

Amma has always set the example of sharing, serving and nourishing. In the early days of the ashram, when we finished sand, cleaning or concrete seva, we would find Amma waiting for us with snacks and black tea. Sometimes, She would serve us a salad of diced apples, guavas and mangos. As soon as we received Her prasad, all the fatigue caused by bodily exertion and the heat would vanish.

During my childhood, my father was working in the Middle East. When I entered my teens, he returned to India and built a new house. I was my parents' only child.

When I turned 17, I accompanied my parents to see Amma in Vallikkavu. My father was a staunch Krishna devotee. He had as much devotion to Amma as he had towards Krishna.

Within a short time, Amma became our Guru. I grew up witnessing my parents' devotion. Their spiritual practices, devotion and faith led me closer to Amma. By the time I completed my college studies, I had made a decision: I wanted to live with Amma.

In hindsight, I don't know if my announcement made my father's face fall or if it saddened him. What I do know is that he went to Amma and said, "Amma, I entrust my daughter to you." When we walked away from that darshan, I saw tears in his eyes. One's eyes well up not only when one is in pain or sorrow; they also well up in the fullness of happiness. That day was an Onam. Amma distributed *pappadam*, banana chips and payasam with the lunch prasad. I loved every moment of it!

In another sense, every day is Onam in Vallikkavu. Onam is a celebration; more than that, it is joyful anticipation. One does not sulk or feel dissatisfied. The festive spirit in Amritapuri becomes slightly dampened only when Amma goes abroad. Even then, She protects the ashram residents from the doldrums by arranging scriptural classes and seva activities. Basking in the joy here, I forgot about my mother and father. In all my time here, they never sought to bind me with cords of attachment, though I was their only child. The fact is, they never ever revealed their sorrows to me.

I would see my parents during Amma's Brahmasthanam festivals in Kodungalloor and Thrissur. They never asked me, "How are you, daughter?" And I never asked them how they were. They passed their time doing some agricultural work in a plot of land they owned. My father's mode of transportation was a bicycle. For these reasons, he never had any serious health problem. After six years in the ashram, Amma entrusted me with school work. The days that followed were busy ones in Amrita Vidyalayam.[1] My world revolved around children, their parents and teachers. I tried to discharge my duties as perfectly as possible.

I only realized that my parents had grown old and that they had been physically unwell after my mother underwent heart surgery, but Amma had all along been inquiring about their well-being and doing all that was necessary. I never knew that.

---

1 Network of schools across India managed by the M.A. Math, and offering value-based education.

The fact is, Amma had looked after and cared for my parents much, much more than I could ever have as a daughter.

In 2015, I returned to Amritapuri from Durgapur (in West Bengal) for the *Guru Purnima* celebrations. By then, my parents had already moved to Amritapuri. Both of them were happy. Plants and agriculture had always been a part of my father's life. He continued doing the same work even after moving to Amritapuri. The only thing I did not see was his bicycle. He was living very happily in Amritapuri.

In 2016, when I went for my room darshan in Amritapuri, Amma spoke to me about my health issues. I realized that She was feeling concerned about the fact that I was living alone, far away from Amritapuri. She said as much, too. After giving room darshan to all the ashram residents, Amma left for the Summer Tour. I returned to Durgapur with my parents, but they didn't like the environment there at all. Coming from Kodungalloor, with its sprawling expanses where they had lived for the better part of their lives, they could not abide by the stifling atmosphere of the office and school. One day, my father told me, "This place isn't working for me... we want to return to the ashram."

I had not told Amma about taking my parents to Durgapur. I sent a message to Amma, who was still touring the U.S. She called and exploded: "Daughter, what do you think you're doing? I was the one who asked them to stay in Amritapuri. To make them travel such a long distance at their age! Escort them back to the ashram immediately. I don't want to hear another word!" With those words, Amma ended the call.

I was in a cold sweat. I realized that I had better act quickly before the next phone call, or things would get out of hand. There was so much school work. But how could I send them back alone? I used to administer insulin injections to my dad. I had no choice but to travel with them. I attended to the pressing matters post-haste and then left for Amritapuri with them.

During the journey, my father told my mother, "If I die in the train, don't inform anyone. You can notify people once we reach Ernakulam."

My father was always joking. I asked him, "Why's that?"

"This body is to be set aside for the students in Amma's medical college," he said.

I asked my mother, "Are you scared of death?"

She laughed and said, "No."

I said, "If we give the body to the medical college, they will cut it up to study it."

Extending her benumbed finger at me, my mother said, "This finger has become numb. I don't feel any sensation."

We reached Amritapuri. My father said, "Now, I feel content!" The next thing I knew, he was distributing the saplings and fruits he had brought from Durgapur. The next day, someone told me, "I saw your father going to the hospital." I did not think there was anything serious. I figured he might have gone to check his blood pressure. I leisurely walked to the hospital. When I reached the hospital, I realized that my father's condition was critical. A nurse was trying to hook him to an intravenous drip. I sat next to my father and started caressing his limbs gently. Soon, more and more brahmacharinis who had heard that my father's condition was deteriorating started arriving. Seeing the cloth bag in my dad's hand, they asked what it was. My father opened his eyes, looked at me, smiled affectionately, and called out "Amma! Amma! ..." He then slowly said, "I saw Amma... I saw Amma..." His eyes closed. With utmost happiness, he left for a world from where there is no return.

Amma was very fond of my father's innocence. I realized that because of his innocence, he had drawn the Guru's grace and compassion. What if we had delayed leaving Durgapur by even one day? What if I had not acted upon Amma's words immediately? I cannot bear to think of the consequences. How sternly Amma had spoken to me that day, insisting that I take my parents back to Amritapuri at once. She knew everything that was going to happen. With how much care and concern the Universal Mother looks after us all.

(February 2017)

Never Too Late

Madhavi (Raymonde Binner), U.S.A.

In July 1994, I met Amma for the first time. It was an incredible experience, an encounter that would change my life forever. I shed many tears of joy.

After the retreat, I visited my family in Québec. Still high from the experience, I was anxious to share it with my family. Soon, joy turned into sadness when my experience was not well received, especially by my mother. She said, "I don't want this Indian woman messing with your brain." She thought I had joined a cult, and was worried about me. She added, "First, you marry a foreigner, then you move to the States, and now this. What's wrong with you?" Consequently, I had to keep quiet about what was most important to me. Only one of my nieces felt some affinity for Amma, and wanted a picture of Her. I gave her one.

In the fall, I dreamt that I was in the bedroom where my mother stays, and I was sweeping and cleaning up old dirt everywhere. Against the wall was a cabin with glass doors through which one could see glass spools of thread arranged in the colors of the rainbow. I asked my mother, "Was this always here?" She said yes. When I woke up from the dream, I had a strong, intuitive feeling that one of us was going to die. The rainbow represented the bridge across to the other world.

As my mother was already 91 years old, I thought most likely it was going to be her — but there was no guarantee. So, that Christmas, I drove to Québec to be with my mother and the rest of the family, thinking it would be our last one together — and it was.

In June 1995, after I returned from a vacation, I called my mother like I usually do. She said to me, "I'm not doing well. I will have to go to a nursing home. When can I see you?" I told her that as I had just returned from my vacation, I would have to work for a couple of weeks, and then I would come.

At the end of June, I drove up. As mother was feeling a bit better, my sister and I took her out of the nursing home for a week and brought her back to her house. Imagine my surprise when I walked into her bedroom and saw a picture of Amma on the headboard. My niece had come for my mother's birthday and had given her the picture of Amma, saying, "Here, this woman can help you!" What a change from a year ago! Amma had gotten here before me, and was already working Her magic. What a relief! I now felt that the door was opened, giving me the opportunity to talk about my experience with Amma.

One night while still in her house, she was not feeling good and was scared to go to sleep. I offered to sleep on the floor in her room. Before we went to sleep, I told her to pray to Amma and that Amma could help her. So she took Amma's picture and said, "You better help me!" I thought, "Well, that's one way of praying when you're scared!" In any case, she slept well that night. I know, because she snored and I did not sleep! The experience gave her the idea that perhaps she could trust Amma and that She could help her.

The next morning, she asked me a question about Amma: "Is she a religion?"

I said, "No, She is all about Love, loving everyone, whether they are healthy or sick, rich or poor, old or young, etc." So she decided to take Amma's picture to the nursing home.

The week that she was in her house, she never said anything sad, depressing or negative. We helped her sort out her clothes to bring with her to the nursing home. It made Amma's teachings about material possessions so relevant: "You can't take them with you." There was something so unreal about her actions, like watching a movie, being detached from the whole thing. Somehow, my sister, my mother and I were going through this without the least bit of sadness; not what I expected from my mother or myself.

One night, she had a dream. We were all together, my sister, my three brothers and my mother, and she told us that she was going to die and asked us not to cry.

At the end of the week, it was time to take her back to the nursing home. As she stepped outside the door, she said, "Oh, I forgot to look around the house." She knew she would never be back. It was a sad moment for me.

In July, I attended the retreat with Amma, and brought a picture of my mother and myself to be blessed. I knew Amma knew that my mother was going to die and that it was my wish to be with her until the end. I felt very sad, cried a lot and started to grieve.

A few weeks later, I returned to Québec to be with my mother. She was diagnosed with lung cancer, and was losing a lot of weight, but was not suffering. She refused chemotherapy and felt blessed that she had lived 92 healthy years, and if this was the way that God wanted to take her, then, so be it.

We started our nightly ritual of praying together while she held Amma's picture on her heart. We would pray for courage, for guidance, for protection, and for Amma to be present. Then, she would tell me, "Go home, get a good night's sleep. I'm fine. I'm not afraid, and I'll see you tomorrow."

One day, I shared my feelings about reincarnation and what Amma has to say about death. She listened intently, but never asked questions. All this was so new to her. Later, she told me how glad she was we had that talk, that it was so helpful, and that my brothers and sister would not have been able to do that.

I once told her, "It must have been very difficult to leave the house that you and dad built and lived in for 60-something years."

She looked at me and said, "No. When I let go, I let go of everything all at once, the house, the TV, the music," and added, "Someone is giving me the courage to do it." This was not my mother talking. She was completely detached and in the moment.

On another occasion, I said, "I'm so proud of you: you're doing this very well — dying, that is."

She answered, "I don't know where it's coming from." I began to suspect that our darling Amma had a hand in all this.

As the end drew near, one day, she said, "This is it, it is time to let go completely, no more fooling around; tomorrow, Sunday, is a good day to die." She started giving instructions as to what dress she would wear (in her coffin), what jewelry, what shoes, who would carry the cross, and who would be the pallbearers. I told her that where she was going, she did not need shoes, she could go barefoot, and she matter-of-factly said, "You're right!" and smiled. She said that we should not disagree about dividing the contents of house, and that she wanted to die with her hands joined, her rosary in the coffin, and a smile on her face. She was totally in charge and acting as if she were dealing with somebody else. She later said it was probably the most difficult decision she had ever made. One does not have the opportunity to practice dying too often. She kept Amma's picture on her heart all night and on her table during the day.

The next morning, it looked like she really was going to die; the change was phenomenal. But she did not. I told her that she had made her reservation to be picked up by God too late and that He would come by on his next trip. She smiled.

On Sunday morning, after she received the last rites, she told us that if we had anything to say to her, it was our last chance. At one point, she motioned my brother, his partner and his ex-wife to come to her bed, grabbed their hands, put them on top of each other as if to say, "It is time to make peace," since they had not spoken to each other for years. It was such a powerful gesture. Everything my mother said and did was definitely not like the mother I knew. The night before she died, I had a very strong intuitive feeling that I should spend the night with her. My wish to be with her until her last breath was fulfilled when she died peacefully at 6 a.m.

Amazingly enough, my mother did have a smile on her face, her hands joined, and her rosary in the coffin — just like she wanted. Because Amma was such a big part of the whole experience, I put Her picture with a small bouquet of wild flowers in the coffin. Many people wanted to know who She was, including the priest. So I had the opportunity to talk about Amma.

My mother's younger sister (then 89) asked me if she could have Amma's picture. I was happy to oblige. She died a couple of years later. Her son then asked me if he could have my aunt's picture of Amma. As far as I know, Amma is still doing Her thing in my family.

Looking back at the whole experience, and with Amma's grace, I learned so much. Through my mother, Amma taught me how to die with courage, with dignity, and without fear — just as She talks about in Her book. Death should be a beautiful experience, and it was. At first, I thought that I would be my mother's teacher, as I had been on a spiritual path for a while — what an ego! It turned out exactly the opposite: my mother became my teacher. Amma had Her plans.

I am so grateful for having taken the time to be with my mother during the last two months of her life. I received many gifts from the experience. First, my fear of death was removed. Second, for the first time in my life, my mother told me that she loved me. Third, because she saw another side of me, she said I was extraordinary — another first. After 58 years of waiting, those words were music to my ears, and I will cherish them for the rest of my life. It was all through Amma's grace.

(July 2010)

Glossary

Acchan — Malayalam word for 'father.'

AIMS — Amrita Institute of Medical Sciences, also referred to as AIMS Hospital, a super-specialty hospital, located in Cochin, Kerala.

Amma — Malayalam word for 'mother.'

Ammuma — Malayalam word for 'grandmother.'

Amrita Vidyalayam — A network of schools across India managed by the M.A. (Mata Amritanandamayi) Math, and offering value-based education.

Amritakuteeram — The M.A. Math's free housing project for the destitute homeless.

Amritanidhi — The M.A. Math's pension scheme for the destitute.

Amritaniketan — An orphanage in Paripally, Kollam, run by the M.A. Math

Amritapuri — International headquarters of the M.A. Math, located at Amma's birthplace in Kerala, India

Amriteshwari — 'Goddess of Immortality,' an epithet associated with Amma

Archana — Chanting of a litany of divine names.

Ashram — Monastery. Amma defines it as a compound: *'aa'*—'that' and *'shramam'*—effort (towards Self-realization)

Ashtottaram — Litany of 108 attributes

Atma — Self or soul

Avadhuta — An enlightened person whose behavior is at odds with social norms.

Avatar — Divine incarnation.

Awaken, Children! — A series of nine books of Amma's conversations, compiled by Swami Amritaswarupananda Puri.

Ayurveda — 'Science of Life;' India's ancient and holistic system of medicine and health; the adjective is 'Ayurvedic.'

Bhagavad Gita	'Song of the Lord,' it consists of 18 chapters of verses in which Lord Krishna advises Arjuna. The advice is given on the battlefield of Kurukshetra, just before the righteous Pandavas fight the unrighteous Kauravas. It is a practical guide to overcoming crises in one's personal or social life, and is the essence of Vedic wisdom.
Bhagavatam	Also known as *Srimad Bhagavatam* or *Bhagavata Purana* (meaning 'Sacred Tales of the Supreme Lord'), one of the Puranic texts of Hinduism. Contains stories of Vishnu, including the life and pastimes of Krishna.
Bhajan	Devotional song or hymn in praise of God.
Bhakti	Devotion for God.
Bhima	Second of the five Pandava brothers, who fought against the Kauravas during the Mahabharata War.
Bindi	Red dot worn on the center of the forehead by Hindu women.
Brahmachari	Celibate male disciple, who practices spiritual disciplines under a Guru's guidance. Brahmacharini is the feminine/female equivalent.
Brahman	Ultimate truth beyond any attribute; the Supreme Reality underlying all life; the divine ground of existence.
Brahmasthanam	'Place of Brahman.' The name of the temples Amma has consecrated in various parts of India and in Mauritius. The temple shrine features a unique four-faced idol that symbolizes the unity behind the diversity of divine forms.
Brahmin	One who belongs to the priestly caste. The four main castes in Indian society are Brahmana (priestly clan), Kshatriya (martial clan), Vaishya (trading community) and Shudra (serving community).

Cent	Unit of measurement still used in Southern India. One cent is equal to an area of a hundredth of an acre (approximately 435.5 square feet).
Dakshina	Honorarium; a donation or payment for the services rendered by a Guru, teacher or priest.
Dakshineswar	Town in Kolkata, West Bengal.
Darshan	Audience with a holy person or a vision of the Divine.
Devi	Goddess / Divine Mother.
Devi Bhava	'Divine Mood of Devi.' The state in which Amma reveals Her oneness and identity with the Divine Mother.
Devi Mahatmyam	700 verses glorifying the Divine Mother.
Diksha	Initiation into a mantra; also known as 'mantra diksha.'
Duryodhana	Eldest of the 100 sons of King Dhritarashtra and Queen Gandhari; leader of the Kaurava clan; and claimant to the throne of Hastinapura.
Ganapati	'Leader of the ganas,' who are Lord Shiva's attendants; another name for Ganesha.
Ganges	India's most sacred river.
Guru	Spiritual teacher.
Guru Purnima	The first full moon night after the summer solstice. On this day, devotees pay homage to their Guru and Sage Vyasa, the compiler of the Vedas, deeply revered by Hindus.
Hari-katha	Narration of sacred tales, especially of Lord Krishna, interspersed with singing of bhajans.
Hatha Yoga	Physical exercises designed to enhance one's overall well-being by toning the body and opening the various channels of the body to promote the free flow of energy.
Homa	Sacred fire ceremony in which the gods are offered oblations.

IAM Integrated Amrita Meditation, a simple combination of yoga, *pranayama* (regulated breathing) and meditation, that Amma originated.

Ishwara Kripa God's grace.

Japa Repeated chanting of a mantra.

Kai-mani Small hand cymbals

Kalari Generally, a center for martial arts training; here, it refers to a temple where Amma used to hold Krishna Bhava and Devi Bhava darshans.

Kali Goddess of fearsome aspect; depicted as dark, wearing a garland of skulls, and a girdle of human hands; feminine of Kala (time).

Kanji Rice gruel.

Karma Action; physical, mental and verbal activity.

Kartika Third constellation, Pleiades; Amma's birth star.

Kathakali Form of dance-drama, native to Kerala.

Kripa Grace

Krishna From 'krish,' meaning 'to draw to oneself' or 'to remove sin;' principal incarnation of Lord Vishnu. He was born into a royal family but raised by foster parents, and lived as a cowherd boy in Vrindavan, where He was loved and worshipped by His devoted companions, the *gopis* (milkmaids) and *gopas* (cowherds). Krishna later established the city of Dwaraka. He was a friend and advisor to His cousins, the Pandavas, especially Arjuna, whom He served as charioteer during the Mahabharata War, and to whom He revealed His teachings as the *Bhagavad Gita*.

Krishna Bhava 'Divine Mood of Krishna,' the state in which Amma reveals Her oneness and identity with Lord Krishna.

Kumbhamela Religious festival that takes place in India once every 12 years, during which Hindus gather to bathe in a sacred river.

Laddu
Indian sweet made from a mixture of flour, sugar and other ingredients that vary according to recipe, and shaped into a ball.

Lakh
Hundred thousand.

Mahatma
'Great soul.' Used to describe one who has attained spiritual realization.

Mala
'Garland.' Strand of beads used for japa.

Malayalam
Language spoken in the Indian state of Kerala.

Mantra
A sound, syllable, word or words of spiritual content.

Matruvani
'Voice of the Mother.' The M.A. Math's flagship publication, which disseminates Amma's teachings through Her messages, essays on spiritual topics, experiences of devotees and disciples, and news reports of the Math's charitable activities, among other topics of spiritual interest. Published in 16 languages, including nine Indian languages (Malayalam, Tamil, Kannada, Telugu, Hindi, Marathi, Gujarati, Bengali and Odiya) as well as English, French, German, Spanish, Italian, Finnish and Japanese, and having a global readership.

Melpattur
Melpattur Narayana Bhattattiri was an erudite scholar who composed the *Narayaneeyam*.

Moksha
Spiritual liberation.

Mudra
Gesture formed by the hands and fingers, and having a mystical import.

Mundu
Garment worn around the waist.

Muruga
'Beautiful one.' One of the names of Kartikeya (child of the Pleiades); second son of Lord Shiva, and brother of Ganapati.

Narayaneeyam
A Sanskrit poem that summarizes the *Bhagavatam*.

Om	Primordial sound in the universe; the seed of creation; the cosmic sound, which can be heard in deep meditation; the sacred mantra, taught in the *Upanishads*, which signifies Brahman, the divine ground of existence; in the meditation that Amma teaches, the sound that one mentally synchronizes with every exhalation during the initial stages of meditation (before the sound dissolves into the breath).
Om namah shivaya	'Salutations to the Auspicious.'
Onam	Kerala's harvest festival.
Ottur Unni Namboodiri	Composer of Amma's Ashtottaram.
Panchamritam	Sweet pudding made from five ingredients.
Panchavadyam	Traditional instrumental ensemble comprising five instruments, typically performing in temples and/or festivals in Kerala.
Paramaguru	Supreme Guru.
Parashakti	Supreme power.
Payasam	Sweet pudding.
Peetham	Sacred chair.
Prarabdha	Consequences of actions done in previous lives that one is destined to experience in the present life.
Prasad	Blessed offering or gift from a holy person or temple, often in the form of food.
Puja	Ritualistic or ceremonial worship.
Pujari	Priest.
Purana	'Ancient (lore).' Hindu folk narratives containing ethical and cosmological teachings relative to Gods, man and the world. They revolve around five subjects: primary creation, secondary creation, genealogy, cycles of time and history. There are 18 major Puranas.
Radha	Milkmaid and beloved companion of Lord Krishna.

Rama	The divine hero of the epic *Ramayana*. An incarnation of Lord Vishnu, He is considered the ideal man of dharma and virtue. *'Ram'* means 'to revel;' one who revels in Himself; the principle of joy within; also one who gladdens the hearts of others.
Ramayana	'Vehicle of Rama.' The tragic love story of Rama and Sita, whose exemplary lives have helped set high standards of dignity and nobility as an integral part of Hindu dharma.
Sadhak	Spiritual aspirant or seeker.
Sadhana	Regimen of disciplined and dedicated spiritual practice that leads to the supreme goal of Self-realization.
Samadhi	Literally, 'cessation of all mental movements;' oneness with God; a transcendental state in which one loses all sense of individual identity; union with Absolute Reality; a state of intense concentration in which consciousness is completely unified.
Samsara	Cycle of births and deaths; the world of flux; the wheel of birth, decay, death and rebirth.
Samskara	The totality of one's personality traits that one has acquired as a result of conditioning over many lifetimes. This can also be taken to mean one's level of inner refinement or character.
Sanctum Sanctorum	'Holy of holies.' The most sacred part of a temple, in which the main icon is installed.
Sankalpa	Divine resolve, usually associated with mahatmas.
Sanyasi	A monk who has taken formal vows of renunciation (*sanyasa*); traditionally wears an ocher-colored robe, representing the burning away of all desires. The female equivalent is sanyasini.

Sanskrit	Ancient Indo-European language; the language of most ancient Hindu scriptures.
Seva	Selfless service, the results of which are dedicated to God.
Satsang	Being in communion with the Supreme Truth. Also being in the company of mahatmas, studying scriptures, listening to a spiritual talk or discussion, and participating in spiritual practices in a group setting.
Shakti	Power; personification of the Universal Mother; principle of pure energy associated with Shiva, the principle of pure consciousness.
Shiva	Worshipped as the first and the foremost in the lineage of Gurus, and as the formless substratum of the universe in relationship to Shakti. He is the Lord of destruction in the Trinity of Brahma (Lord of Creation), Vishnu (Lord of Sustenance), and Maheshvara (Shiva).
Sishya	Disciple
Sri Lalita Sahasranama	Sacred litany of 1,000 names of Sri Lalita Devi, the Supreme Goddess.
Sri Mata Amritanandamayi Devi	Amma's official monastic name, meaning 'Mother of Immortal Bliss.'
Sri Ramakrishna Paramahamsa	19th century spiritual master from West Bengal, hailed as the apostle of religious harmony. He generated a spiritual renaissance that continues to touch the lives of millions.
Sri Ramana Maharshi	Enlightened spiritual master (1879 – 1950) who lived in Tiruvannamalai in Tamil Nadu. He recommended Self-inquiry as the path to Liberation, though He approved of a variety of paths and spiritual practices.
Sri Sharada Devi	Consort of Sri Ramakrishna Paramahamsa.

Sudhamani	'Ambrosial jewel,' name that Amma's parents gave Her.
Swami	Title of one who has taken the vow of sanyasa.
Tulasi	Holy basil.
Upanishad	The portions of the Vedas dealing with Self-knowledge.
Vallickavu	Village across the backwaters on the eastern side of the peninsula where the Amritapuri Ashram is located. Amma is sometimes referred to as 'Vallikkavu Amma' or 'Vallickavil Amma.'
Vedanta	'The end of the Vedas.' It refers to the *Upanishads*, which deal with the subject of Brahman, the Supreme Truth, and the path to realize that Truth.
Vedas	Most ancient of all scriptures, originating from God, the Vedas were not composed by any human author but were 'revealed' in deep meditation to the ancient seers. These sagely revelations came to be known as Vedas, of which there are four: *Rig*, *Yajus*, *Sama* and *Atharva*.
Vibhuti	Sacred ash.
Yashoda	Foster mother of Krishna.
Yoga	From *'yuj'* (*samadhau*), which means 'to concentrate the mind;' *'yuj'* (*samyamane*), which means 'to control;' and *'yujir'* (*yoge*), which means 'to unite.' Union with the Supreme Being. A broad term, it also refers to the various methods of practices through which one can attain oneness with the Divine. A path that leads to Self-realization.

CPSIA information can be obtained
at www.ICGtesting.com
Printed in the USA
LVHW082109010519
616153LV00009BA/50/P